To my wife, Clare, for making every day more fun

THE YEAR OF
THE TIGER

HarperCollins books may be purchased for educational, business, or sales promotional use. For information, please email the Special Markets Department at SPsales@harpercollins.com.

FIRST EDITION

Designed by Kyle O'Brien
Title page art © Tint Media/Shutterstock

Library of Congress Cataloging-in-Publication Data has been applied for.

ISBN 978-0-06-341812-7

25 26 27 28 29 LBC 5 4 3 2 1

THE YEAR OF
THE TIGER

———

*The Major Run
That Made Tiger Woods*

BRODY MILLER

HARPER

An Imprint of HarperCollinsPublishers

CONTENTS

CONTENTS

THE YEAR OF
THE TIGER

INTRODUCTION

There he stood, doing the impossible, infuriated with the mistakes that he'd made. There was Tiger Woods, yes, but not the Tiger Woods you remember. His face was more worn. His lower body moved less. He did not have a Nike swoosh on his shirt or hat but instead his own new company logo.

Woods was forty-eight, standing in a fairway of a place that immortalized him, hitting an approach into 18 to make the cut at the 2024 Masters. The crowd around him no longer expected greatness. They were not there to see him storm back from behind for victory. They were not there for him to put his iron shot near the pin. Nothing that day was about how Woods played. It was about the fact he was playing. Thousands of patrons swarmed around him at Augusta National not to see him play great, but to see greatness.

Woods hit his approach and stared up at the sky with hope. He did not know where it would go or how it would land. It was just hope. And as he saw it fly left, bouncing off the edge of the green to the fairway, his face scrunched. He was sickened. He quietly mouthed an expletive to himself and stared down at his body. He held that stare, his eyes just disappointingly glaring at the body beneath him, longing for some different set of pieces to help him hit the ball. The mind of Tiger Woods was still in there, and that made it worse. Because the mind was all too aware of the body that betrayed it.

His back was fused. His ankle was, too. His leg was a piece of machinery filled with hardware and alterations. If he was wearing shorts, you'd see the gruesome scars, too, constant reminders that he was not supposed to be on this fairway. The scars were from the horrific rollover car crash three years before on the side of Hawthorne Boulevard. His car was torn to pieces. As was his leg. He was lucky to be alive, and right then people stopped wondering whether Woods would pass Jack Nicklaus' records or play competitive golf. They simply wondered if he'd be able to play with his kids again.

But the humor—or perhaps the sadness—in Woods' disgust was the reason for it. He was a forty-eight-year-old, surgically repaired contraption that had no business still being here. Each step was followed by a strong limp. Most shots were met with grimaces. Yet as his shot missed the green, he remained five shots clear of the 36-hole cut line. He got up and down for par and made history with his twenty-fourth consecutive made cut at the Masters, the longest streak in history. Still, despite everything that happened in the past twenty-eight years of his Shakespearian story, he never once missed the Masters cut as a professional.

But remember, that was still the mind of Tiger Woods in there, and that mind had zero interest in becoming a ceremonial golfer.

"I still think I can win," he'd tell anyone who asked.

Because he still remembers the roars. He remembers the shots that exceeded belief. He remembers what it felt like to hit a ball so pure, to enter any tournament knowing he should win, to accomplish things no golfer ever had. And until that memory fades, Woods is not wired to accept anything less.

This book is about that mind as much as the body. It's

about a teenager who thought he could win more majors than anyone in history. It's about a twenty-one-year-old wondering about winning four majors in a row. It's about a human being who had all the expectation and pressure in the world on him, and somehow he exceeded it.

In 2000 and on through April 2001, Woods didn't just play excellent golf. He crossed a threshold from the player with the most ability to the fully actualized legend capable of anything.

This is not an origin story. Those have been told countless times. And it is not a deep dive into his decline. There are many well-reported pieces on that fall. It is a book about the nexus point in time when the person who is *supposed* to become something actually makes that final step to live inside those expectations. It is not about how Bruce Wayne became Batman. It's about Batman saving Gotham.

In telling the story of Woods' greatest achievement and the greatest year in golf history—when he won all four professional majors in a row from June 2000 to April 2001—we combined interviews with those there for the most important and intimate moments with the never-ending source texts chronicling the time. The benefit and challenge of writing about Woods is that he is one of the most sought-after and intriguing American figures of the past century. In turn, Woods does not grant one-on-one interviews anymore, especially not for books about him. So, Woods declined to speak to us for *The Year of the Tiger.* On the other hand, Woods' entire life, from his childhood to his daily golf life to his dating life and beyond, is so intensely covered that there is an incessant well of interviews, articles, and documents to use to tell these stories. There are also figures along for the ride who love to speak about this time, like his longtime coach Butch Harmon. There are those who wrote memoirs going into depth on each moment, like his father, Earl, his caddie Steve Williams, or his other swing coach Hank Haney. And there are the competitors who looked the tiger in the eye and have tall tales to tell, from rivals like Phil Mickelson, David Duval, and Ernie Els to shocking Cinderellas like Bob May and Chris DiMarco. It is in the collision of all these sources that this narrative can be formed.

This book is not intended to be a mere recollection of exciting moments but an investigation into that moment in time when Eldrick Tont Woods truly, for better or worse, turned into Tiger. It is a study into the decisions and factors that can take a figure from the next big thing to the *only* thing, and it's a cautionary tale for how those same traits can be cause for glory and reason for collapse.

Because thousands of people still crowd him along the galleries at Augusta National, hoping to catch a glimpse of the most iconic figure of their time. They are well aware that they likely won't see the version of him that created such fanfare. But to be able to say you saw Woods in person still carries weight. They know he will not always be there to see.

And it's in these pages that we can go back and remember why we still seek out a glimpse of Tiger Woods. The accomplishments are not just text in a record book or clips of a famous fist pump. They were moments in time, and few created more moments than him.

―――――

Chapter One

TIGER WOODS
HAS A PROBLEM

The greatest golf season of all time was just beginning, and Tiger Woods had only one golf ball left
in his bag.

He didn't know it. The world didn't know it. The only
person who knew was a well-built Kiwi who was having a
quiet yet significant panic attack a few feet away. Woods
was blissfully unaware, standing along the California
coastline, cursing his own failure to achieve actual perfection. This was typical. The game's best golfer had a

seven-shot lead at the US Open, and he couldn't forgive himself for losing a stroke.

That Saturday morning drive off the 18th tee and into the water at Pebble Beach Golf Links would have no real impact on who won the major championship. The only thing that could bring Woods down and within reach of the mere mortals that week was that last golf ball—or, really, all the other ones, which were missing.

Caddie Steve Williams stood behind Woods, fighting with all of his considerable strength to keep the fear he felt from showing. What if Woods hit another ball into the water? What if he ran out of balls at the damn US Open? Williams imagined every terrible scenario. The job he'd surely lose. The international pariah he'd become.

As far as Williams knew, he was about to cost Woods the tournament.

Woods avoided locker rooms in those days. It bothered the other pros, but he was always worried somebody could tamper with his gear or steal his prized possession, his Scotty Cameron Newport 2 GSS putter.

He liked to call himself a "car-park pro," going back to the old days of him playing youth and college golf out of the back of his car with all his gear in there ready to play at any moment. Williams called it a "self-deprecating game" Woods played with himself to remember his humble beginnings. But at Pebble Beach, Woods stayed at the lodges on the course and didn't have a car. So, after darkness ended play on Friday, midway through the second round as Woods held a six-shot lead, Williams brought Woods' golf bag to his room at the lodge. There were six balls in there at the time. When he arrived the next day, the bag was right where he left it, so Williams didn't think anything of it and took off for the range. Because of the early restart, they didn't have time for their full pre-round routine of going to the driving range, back to the putting green, and then to the course. They had to skip the putting green.

But as they approached the 13th tee and prepared to finish the round, Williams looked in the bag to find only three balls.

Where were the other three? Well, Woods wanted to practice his putting after the round, but it was too dark to use the practice green. Alone in the lodge, he took out three balls and practiced putting on the floor. He never put them away, and Williams didn't notice them sitting on the floor in the wee hours of the morning.

As Williams did finally notice, he decided to keep his mouth shut. It wouldn't help anything to tell Tiger. There were only six holes to play, and something would have to go very wrong for Woods to lose all three.

That was until they walked along on the side of the 14th green and Woods tossed a ball to a young fan. There was a scuff mark on the ball, so Woods had no problem giving it to the kid. Williams' heart sank. This kid was over the moon, and Williams wrestled with whether he should try to get the ball back. How would he even do it? He considered making a deal with him to offer a box of balls on 18 for this one back. He decided that was a bad idea.

"Figured it wouldn't be a good look if Tiger Woods' caddie took a ball off a happy kid. There'd be tears for sure."

Williams scanned the gallery for a member of Woods' entourage to go run to the lodge and grab more balls, but it was so early that nobody was there. They had two balls left, and Woods was dialed in. His lead was eight shots. He played the next three holes safely, and all seemed to be OK.

But 18 at Pebble Beach is a long, 543-yard par 5 with the Pacific Ocean lining the entire fairway and green. It is a forgiving fairway, but in the back of the mind of each and every golfer on the tee are the massive waves brushing against the rocks along the sea wall. There was zero reason for Woods not to hit driver. But it still made Williams nervous as Woods asked, "Do you like driver?"

Again, Williams kept his mouth shut and handed him the driver. And amid arguably the greatest four rounds of golf ever played, Woods hooked his drive left into the water. Woods went on a cursing rant, shouting, "Goddamn you fucking prick!" and eventually saying, "Give me another fucking ball."

Williams handed Woods the final ball, but he put the driver back in the bag with his hand covering it. It was his little, not-so-subtle way of saying not to hit the big club again. Perhaps he'd like to hit a 2-iron and play for safety?

"Take your fucking hand off that," Woods said.

There Woods was, the greatest player in the world, about to run away with a US Open, completely unaware he was one more bad shot away from a major penalty for running out of balls. It could have been one of the greatest gaffes in golf history. Williams was behind him mapping out strategies for sprinting the five hundred yards, getting up to the room, and grabbing more balls. You're allowed five minutes. He probably wasn't that fast. He practically shook as Woods hit the tee shot, fully prepared to lose his job. As far as Williams knew, Woods would be disqualified.

Woods hit the fairway, of course. He ultimately bogeyed the hole and got into the clubhouse with a six-shot lead with thirty-six holes to go. It wasn't until later Williams learned it only would have been a two-shot penalty if he had to run and get more balls. He still thinks it would have been enough to lose his job.

He didn't tell Tiger that night. He saved that for when they both could laugh about it.

For the moment, Tiger had the lead, and golf's greatest run was underway.

———

No matter what happened next or what was really on the line that morning along Carmel Bay, just remember the ways we take the greatest moments in history as givens. That's because we know they already happened, like rewatching a movie where we know the ending.

Nobody had ever won four professional majors in a row. Tiger Woods had to start with the first one. Hundreds and thousands of tiny little moments, coincidences, and decisions compiled to allow each of these victories to become each and every little victory on the ride. If any of those minuscule moments didn't happen, this breakthrough might not exist.

If you are reading this book, you are likely well aware of Tiger Woods. You know of the 15 major championships, the 82 PGA Tour wins, and the 683 total weeks as world No. 1, more than double the golfer with the second most time at the top. You might know he was the youngest golfer to win the U.S. Junior Amateur and then won it three years in a row. Or that he was the youngest U.S. Amateur winner and then won that three years in a row, too. You know he won the 1997 Masters in his first attempt as a professional by twelve shots at just twenty-one years old. You know he was the youngest golfer to achieve the career Grand Slam, won fourteen majors by age thirty-two, and overcame significant physical and personal hardship to return eleven years later with a win at the 2019 Masters. And, if you're reading a book about the Tiger Slam, you likely know he is the only golfer to ever consecutively win all four majors open to professionals, as he did from June 2000 to April 2001. There will always remain debate whether Woods or Jack Nicklaus is golf's all-time greatest. Nicklaus won eighteen majors in his career, marking a milestone that Woods hasn't been able to pass. But even Nicklaus has admitted Woods was the best and most dominant golfer to ever play the sport at his peak.

Nobody, not even Nicklaus, can match the feat Woods

achieved from June 15, 2000, to April 8, 2001. Four major championships were played in those ten months. Tiger won all four. He won the 2000 US Open at Pebble Beach, the 2000 Open Championship at St Andrews, the 2000 PGA Championship in Louisville via a dramatic playoff, and the 2001 Masters. It is, and very likely will always be, the only time a golfer has ever held all four professional majors at once. And while we'll get into the semantics of whether this qualifies a true Grand Slam, at the very least, history will always give Woods his own chapter: the Tiger Slam.

When discussing the most iconic and lore-filled athletes in American history, Woods sits on an exclusive list of legends like Michael Jordan, Babe Ruth, and Muhammad Ali. He is not simply a great athlete who mastered a sport. He is the type talked about with folktales and myths, both in his stunning highs and his ensuing downfall. He is the great sports *character* of his time.

From the moment he first showed up on television as a two-year-old boy putting against Bob Hope on *The Mike Douglas Show* through him winning the Masters at twenty-one, Woods *was* a seemingly superhuman prodigy with no real comparison in sports. And from 1999 to 2008, he reached a level of absolute supremacy none thought possible. Maybe the only realistic similarities for that kind of childhood are Michael Jackson and Mozart, not athletes. LeBron James became national news as a high school teenager. Lionel Messi was sixteen when he first ran on the pitch for Barcelona. Serena Williams won her first Grand Slam before she was twenty. But to have the whole world know you as a toddler, to have people talking about how many majors you'll win before you can drive a car, and then to actually exceed expectations? The only others with that kind of childhood pressure didn't last. Eventually, Woods fell from grace, too.

To actually understand what Woods achieved from 1999 to 2001, to comprehend the significance of the Tiger Slam, we have to go back to a twenty-three-year-old Woods under constant scrutiny. He had one major championship. He had briefly fallen to No. 3 in the world. It was understood that Woods might be the best player in the field, but the claims that he was superhuman were turning into punch lines.

After he won the 1997 Masters at twenty-one, he won two more tournaments but finished 12th in the Tour Championship. He didn't finish better than 19th at the final three majors, and many in golf circles were more than happy to tear down the guy they'd been told was better than them before he played a professional round.

"Tiger is proving to be a lot like everybody else on the PGA Tour," Greg Norman said at the end of 1997. "Tiger got off to a phenomenal fast start. But he's come back to reality, and he's just another golfer out there."

He won once in 1998, only adding to the questions. To be clear, he was still fourth on the PGA Tour money list and remained world No. 1 as a twenty-two-year-old star, but that was looked on as a quasi-failure to someone with Woods' expectations. Fellow players had to listen to talk of each tournament being "Tiger vs. the field," and peers like Ernie Els scoffed and criticized writers who'd suggest such a thing.

It didn't help that a twenty-six-year-old American named David Duval seemed to pass Woods. Duval was born onto a golf course as the son of a Jacksonville club pro. He attended Georgia Tech and got off to a solid, steady start to his career before breaking out in 1997. He won the Tour Championship to cap off a three-win campaign, and then in 1998 he won four more tournaments before overtaking Woods as world No. 1 with two wins in January 1999. Davis Love III even passed Woods at No. 2. Press conferences around that time were filled with questions for Woods about Duval, and Woods could recall shots by Duval in detail and discuss his game like he studied it. The so-called rivalry became enough of a talking point in 1999 that ABC built a program around a match between Woods and Duval. It was the start of a long-running series called

Monday Night Golf, and that first match earned a 6.9 rating that made it the second-most-watched golf event of the year behind only the Masters.

Sports are filled with talents who break in at a young age. That in and of itself is not groundbreaking. Nicklaus had three majors by Woods' age in 1999. After Woods came other prodigies, like Jordan Spieth winning three majors by twenty-three. Rory McIlroy had two majors by twenty-three and four by twenty-five. When McIlroy won that fourth major at the 2014 PGA Championship, the popular analytics website FiveThirtyEight published a piece suggesting McIlroy might be more likely to pass Nicklaus than Woods. Neither Spieth nor McIlroy have won another in the near decade since.

It isn't the early rise that sets the greatest apart. It's the moment when they meet those expectations and take another leap, passing a threshold few were even considering.

Woods was behind all of those other golfers' paces in 1999, and by all indications he might level off like most do. But there was a clear reason for this supposed slump that was not completely understood at the moment. That two-year stretch was a time of change. He changed caddies. He changed agents. And he was changing something else, something that tells us so much more about Tiger Woods.

———

Chapter Two

TIGER 2.0

Whoosh. Thud. Open. *Food.*
  Whoosh. Thud. Open. *Food.*

It's on repeat in that moment and for eternity, more than the father could ever know. The father stands on the striped carpet in the snug garage, a small patch of turf in the center as he swings his 5-iron and whips golf balls into a net he rigged in his Cypress, California, home. There are boxes lining the garage along both sides. There's an exercise bike a foot behind him. It's 1976. Gerald Ford is in the White House. Orange County is a white, conservative enclave where Richard Nixon set up a hideaway. And in this garage, a mixed-race family whose origins span four continents set their six-month-old son up in a high chair to watch the father "stripe" balls on repeat until the game is so ingrained in the boy that it's the only refuge he can find.

Earl Woods is a forty-four-year-old Vietnam veteran who works his job for a defense contractor, comes home, and escapes straight to his sanctuary to have a drink, smoke a cigarette, and pour himself into his actual passion: golf. He wasn't a particularly good father to the three children from his first marriage. He neglected them and walked out on their mother. But now he has this six-month-old named Eldrick Tont Woods. You can call him Tiger. Tiger sits in the high chair, immersed. He can't stop staring at the swing, the whoosh, the thud, looking over to the net to see where it lands. The mother tries to take him out of the high chair to feed him, but he refuses. "Uh-uh," the boy mutters with sass.

Kultida Woods has to bring the baby food to the garage with a spoon in hand. The thirty-two-year-old Thai mother is also in this garage because of Earl Woods. She was a secretary and receptionist at the U.S. Army office in Bangkok when Lt. Col. Earl Woods entered her life in 1967. Soon she moved to New York with him. Then California. Then came the child. And this stubborn boy won't stop watching his father swing a golf club across a turf patch on a carpet. She has to feed him between shots.

The boy becomes so focused and so trained that he watches Earl swing, watches the ball, opens his mouth, and the mother inserts the food into his mouth. He swallows. Then watches another swing. Then opens his mouth. Then receives more food. So, from the earliest days of his life, Tiger Woods is classically conditioned to associate a golf swing with nourishment. A good swing and a reward.

No, he will not go on to remember these moments. He is not even a year old. But neuroscientific studies have been published for decades on the effects of repetitive stimuli on a young child. Some argue conditioning can be established even *days* after birth. And in this instance, Pavlov's bell is a golf swing. It is practice. It is perfection.

So, it's twenty-three years later and there Woods is— practicing. Alone. It's not in a garage this time but on a driving range. This is the place that for the rest of his life he calls his sanctuary. It is where he can find peace away from the fame and pandemonium of being Tiger Woods. It is where he can connect with the most foundational parts of who he is and where this all began.

Something happens. It's 1999. The twenty-three-year-old phenom in the midst of handling criticism and astronomical expectations finds something. He picks up the phone and immediately calls his swing coach, Butch Harmon.

"Butchie, I got it."

Golf would never be the same.

———

After Woods won the Masters in 1997, he flew off to Mexico and partied. He even blew off a Bill Clinton invitation to a ceremony honoring Jackie Robinson because he felt the invitation arrived at the last second only because he won (an incident he later wrote to Robinson's widow, Rachel, apologizing for). But Woods was also exhausted from a wild year and a wild life all seemingly leading to that moment. He needed a release. "I do know how to have fun," Woods joked in his 2001 instructional book *How I Play Golf.* He spent four days in Mexico, eating and drinking with old friends from high school and college. "I knew I would have to come back to earth eventually," Woods said, "but I wasn't in any special hurry to get there."

One day, about a week or so later, Woods went to the Golf Channel headquarters in Orlando and put in the film of his final round at Augusta. He was alone with no distractions, allowing him to concentrate and home in on critiquing his swing to find an area to improve on. That's how Woods thinks. But as he watched what was supposedly the high-water mark of his career, he became sick to his stomach.

"I didn't see one flaw," Woods said. "I saw about ten . . . I had gotten away with murder."

His club shaft came across the line at the top of his backswing. His clubface was closed. His swing plane was too upright. The ball flight was pretty good, but he was hitting it farther with his irons than he should because he was delofting the clubface through impact. At least that's how Woods saw it. These were all issues Harmon had been pointing out to him for a while, but this was the first time Woods really saw them. Or at least the first time he felt motivated to address them. "I didn't like the look of those things," he said, "and the more I thought about it, the more I realized I didn't like how my swing felt either." He called Harmon and decided it was time to get to work.

The entire world envied Tiger Woods' swing, and he was going to change it.

Harmon wanted to address the issues one problem at a time, little by little. Woods wanted to go radical. He insisted on fixing everything right away. That way he could test it during tournaments and play through the year with it. Maybe within that was a luxury only somebody like Woods could afford. He had such aspirations that he was not worrying about what would make him the best golfer in 1998. He was thinking about what would make him the best for twenty years.

"Anybody can time their golf swing for a week at this level," Woods said at the time. "Anybody can do that. But now, to time it for an entire career, there's no way I could do that with that golf swing."

Making that decision in the moment takes courage. Sticking with it when things aren't going well is another thing. As he only won once in 1998, the press eventually picked up on the swing change. That meant more questions. More scrutiny. To compare it to the modern era, Norwegian golfer Viktor Hovland ended the 2023 season as arguably the best golfer in the world after winning the BMW Championship and Tour Championship in consecutive weeks before thriving at the Ryder Cup. Many argued he was surpassing world No. 1 Scottie Scheffler. But Hovland, a notoriously process-obsessed tinkerer, decided to change much of his swing at twenty-five years old because he didn't like how he was hitting the ball. He didn't win a single tournament in 2024 and had the worst overall season of his career. Talk shifted toward whether Hovland's tinkering could cost him an incredible future, and he wasn't near the level of Woods.

"But in Tiger's case, it was never anything that he felt was not going to be the right thing to do," Harmon said. "He knew the deeper changes he had to make."

Deeper within this search for perfection is a need for something else to chase. There is a compulsiveness driving so many great athletes from Jordan to Tom Brady to Bill Russell, but the origins of such compulsiveness are debated and likely impossible for us to know without truly knowing each detail of their life and DNA. By most biographical accounts of Woods' childhood, in particular the exhaustively reported *Tiger Woods* by Jeff Benedict and Armen Keteyian, Woods grew up in a cold, unsentimental home in Cypress. Especially once Earl and Kultida learned how talented Woods was at a young age, most of his early years were spent in a focused, goal-driven environment. Each parenting decision was about ensuring Woods lived up to his potential. The Benedict and Keteyian biography even suggests Woods' parents drove his high school and college girlfriend Dina Gravell out of the picture because she was a distraction, and Gravell spoke of the stark differences between her loving home, where Woods spent time and ate dinner with her parents, and the sterilized nature of the Woods home, filled with trophies and ambition.

Earl was a military man using psychological tricks to create a golfing robot unaffected by any outside influence. Most of Woods' early years were spent at the Navy Golf Course in Cypress with Earl doing anything and everything to ruffle Woods' feathers. He'd jingle change while he played, drop his clubs in the middle of Woods' swing, or walk directly in his putting line. He'd hurl insults at him and call him every name in the book. The rule was anything goes, and he couldn't talk back or complain. Although there was a code word they agreed on that Woods could use if he ever wanted it to stop.

"Don't ask me how or why—perhaps it was stubbornness—but I never used it," he said.

Kultida, according to many close to Woods, was an unflinchingly attentive mother but also the one who instilled Woods' vicious competitiveness. "Her philosophy was you put your foot on their throats," family friend Pete McDaniel said. Woods later recalled, "She was very strict. She said if I ever crossed the boundaries that she set, there was always consequences."

Many psychiatrists and neuroscientists correlate compulsive perfectionism to home lives or personal relationships. Psychiatrist David Burns found it often comes from the fear of rejection or inadequacy. Harry Stack Sullivan connected it to "insecurity and uncertainty that result from growing up in an unloving household." Leon Salzman of Georgetown University School of Medicine found that the problem is often not the hostile impulses but the need to be loved and accepted.

Woods developed a speech impediment in his youth, with a doctor suggesting it came from the confusion of hearing English and Thai in the home. He wrote in *The 1997 Masters: My Story*: "My stuttering was so noticeable, and it made me feel so anxious that I made sure to sit at the back of the classroom hoping that my teachers wouldn't call on me." Talking about golf was the only time his confidence grew, and on the course itself was where he found value. He took two years of after-school speech lessons, and his parents bought him a Labrador retriever named Boom-Boom. He'd hole up in his bedroom talking to Boom-Boom until he fell asleep.

"I was an only child, and the club and ball became my playmates," Woods said. "That feeling of solitude and self-reliance enhanced the game's attraction for me and endures today."

He went on to write: "While other kids were stuck inside on bad-weather days in a state of boredom, I was being entertained by golf. I turned our living room into a chipping area. I would hit flop shots off the carpet over the coffee table and land the ball short of the fireplace. I never broke anything although I came close a few times. People are always asking me about the pressure of tournament golf. I'll let you in on a little secret. I had to hit those floppers so they made little or no noise because if Mom had heard me hitting balls in her living room," she would not have been happy, he joked.

"The pressure of tournament golf pales in comparison."

———

Tiger's first golf teacher was Rudy Duran at Heartwell Golf Course in Long Beach. Then came John Anselmo, a well-respected California coach in his sixties who steered Woods through his junior amateur stardom until Anselmo was diagnosed with colon cancer in 1993. Earl sought out finding a new coach to take Woods to *another* level, and he homed in on the man who developed Greg Norman's swing to become the best in the world. That man was Butch Harmon.

Back then, Harmon was director of golf at Lochinvar Golf Club in Houston, and Woods was in town to play the

1993 U.S. Amateur. Harmon invited him to come by and put on a little exhibition, and of course Woods wowed the coaching legend with the speed and power in his swing mixed with the creativity and precision.

Harmon asked him, "Tiger, everybody has a stock shot when they want to drive the fairway. Maybe hit it a little lower, hit a little fade or draw. What's your go-to shot?"

Woods, as Harmon recalls, didn't have one. "Nah, I just hit it as far as I can and go find it."

"Well, there's a cocky little sonofabitch," he thought to himself. But over time he learned it wasn't quite cockiness. That was just how he played. They spent three hours together that Saturday. Then he invited Woods and his father, Earl, to come back Sunday, too. A week later, Harmon got a call from Earl. "I think I've taken Tiger about as far as I can take him. Would you like to be his coach?"

Harmon would, and he understood the Woods family didn't have much money, so he agreed not to charge them until Woods went pro and had success. Then he'd send a bill (which he did). Thus began an iconic cross-country relationship, with Harmon buying Woods a camcorder and having them film Woods' game and then FedExing the film to Houston. They'd then discuss what he saw over the phone. Harmon had just one request when Earl asked him to take over.

"This isn't going to work if I have him doing something and you try to get him to do something else," Harmon said.

"I'll make a deal with you," Earl said. "You don't try to be his father and I won't try to be his coach."

They thrived together, winning three U.S. Amateurs and a Masters in the next four years. Then came the mandate to fix his swing, and the duo got to work. "Anything he wasn't good at, he worked his ass off to get good at it," Harmon said. "When he was the best player in the world, which he was for longer than anybody, he worked harder than anyone else. He was gonna stay there. He was never satisfied."

When the famous "I got it" call arrived in 1999, it was because after all the work they put in, it was finally feeling natural to Woods. Golf is such a mental game that the moment you're swinging without complete confidence, you're compromised. Woods was playing solid, world-class golf without that comfort. Suddenly it was back. He flew to Germany for the Deutsche Bank-SAP Open and won against five of the top ten players in the world. Two weeks later, he was in Ohio at Jack Nicklaus' Muirfield Village, one of the bigger stops on tour, and shot 15-under par to run away with the win. He sat up at the winners' press conference with Nicklaus and opened by saying:

"As I told everybody last year, that I'm making these changes and it's just a matter of being patient with them. People were saying, 'Oh, geez, you're not winning, you're not being consistent,' but the press was all over me last year about it, especially with David playing well. I knew the changes I was making in my game were going to be beneficial down the long haul. Knowing that I just had to be patient with it. Over the last couple weeks, it's really starting to come together. Winning in Germany, then winning here, in the last two starts, definitely makes you feel pretty good."

He said he was "starting to understand how to play," that he had more shots in his arsenal, that he was more creative. It was just one PGA Tour win, but it set off alarms. Nicklaus added, "I don't know if anybody can play the way he plays. That's the point I'm saying. He has the ability to do things that nobody else can do."

Here was a new Tiger Woods. He had been hitting the gym, because he had to get stronger to make many of the swing changes. He came on tour at 158 pounds. Soon he was closer to 180. But that strength didn't necessarily get used for power. It was used for complete control of his swing. And that control meant more sustainability and reliability. He went from averaging 320 yards in 1997 to 300, but the unpredictability faded. His fairways hit percentage went from 97th to the top 50 while still hitting much farther than most of his peers.

Woods also said he understood how to be a pro better than he did in 1997. As an amateur, his entire year was essentially constructed around winning the U.S. Amateur. Nobody was better at working their game to peak at the biggest competitions, but as a pro he had four majors, not one. Then he had important tour events in between. "When I first came out, I was still struggling with that," he said. "I was only used to playing three, four months, that's about it. Playing tournaments once a month. It's a little different schedule playing all year long. And I got a little worn out in '97, I didn't schedule it properly." By 1999 he had nailed all that down, and new agent Mark Steinberg was whittling down Woods' schedule away from golf to ensure he wasn't worn down.

It was a time of constant change.

———

Steve Williams was ready to retire well before all the drama with missing golf balls. Sure, he was only thirty-five, but he'd spent a life carrying bags. He started caddying at his home course in New Zealand at age six. By ten, he was caddying thirty-six holes on Saturday and Sunday, then practicing his own game until dark. He wasn't even thirteen when he impressed five-time Open Championship winner Peter Thomson enough at the New Zealand Open that Thomson used Williams whenever he returned to New Zealand. He'd travel to Australia on school breaks to get more work, and by sixteen he was off caddying full-time on the European Tour. Ian Baker-Finch gave him steady work, and Greg Norman used him as his caddie in Australian and Asian events for seven years before Williams moved to the U.S. in 1988 to do it full time. After a breakup with Norman that Williams said was because they became "too close," he spent the next decade working for the aging four-time major champ Raymond Floyd. It was a heck of a career.

Williams was confident and direct. He wasn't afraid to call a golfer off his shot or disagree with him, especially in pressure situations. But he was fiercely loyal and saw it as his job to protect the golfer from outside noise. Plus, he was simply good at being a caddie. He was one of the best at yardage and club selection. He was even good at handling weather, avidly reading *The Old Farmer's Almanac*. He claimed he became a barometer for other caddies, because if Williams wasn't carrying an umbrella, they didn't need to either.

Williams knew Woods, of course, but not well. His boss, Floyd, eventually became one of Woods' favorite mentors and go-to pairings to play Augusta National with. He loved picking the veterans' brains and hearing old war stories. As an amateur, he played a practice round at the 1996 Masters with Floyd, Norman, and Fred Couples. Williams saw this skinny little kid he'd heard could launch it past the best in the game.

His first drive he sure did hit it far, but he also sliced it so far into the trees they didn't know just *how* far he hit it. On the second hole at Augusta—a famous dogleg left par 5 called Pink Dogwood—there's a large bunker on the right side of the fairway that only the longest have to worry about. On this chilly morning with heavy moisture in the air, it definitely didn't seem reachable to the pros. Woods turned to his caddie.

"Can I fly that bunker?" he asked.

Williams and everyone in the group smirked at each other. Good luck, they thought.

Then Woods stepped to the tee, and the twenty-year-old amateur launched a drive over the bunker and into the fairway. A deathly silence overcame the group, their mouths open in amazement. "These legends of the game were dumbstruck, and the silence was broken only when Tiger cracked a joke as we all walked off the tee with our tails between our legs," Williams said.

But three years later, Williams was ready to retire. It was the 1999 Doral-Ryder Open, and Williams and Floyd stood on the practice green talking about the end of their ride. Floyd was fifty-six, his career riding down. And Williams had decided he liked the idea of caddying through the century and calling it quits in 2000.

Little did he know that the best player in the world needed a caddie.

Woods was in the process of parting ways with the beloved fifty-one-year-old celebrity caddie Mike "Fluff" Cowan. Fluff stood out on a golf course. He was a Grateful Dead obsessive with a big, droopy mustache and a hippie vibe. He started caddying for Woods at his 1996 professional debut at the Milwaukee Open and they had been together since, and that sore-thumb aesthetic in tandem with the most famous golfer in the world meant Cowan became more famous than many of the players. He starred in "This is *SportsCenter*" commercials and was dating a much younger woman. Tiger reportedly didn't like all this attention on Cowan, and it reached a head when Cowan broke a major rule for caddies. In a caddie roundtable with *Golf Digest*, he disclosed how much Woods was paying him: $1,000 a week plus 10 percent of winnings. That set Woods off, and the week it published Woods was already asking Harmon for replacement suggestions. One of those was Williams.

The only thing that's unclear is if Floyd already knew all this as they talked about their retirements on the practice green that day at Doral. Was he just playing dumb? Because at some point that week, Harmon broached Floyd with the topic of Woods hiring Williams out of respect. Floyd said he'd think about it. Woods wasn't patient enough.

Wednesday, the night before the tournament, Williams' phone rang in his hotel room.

"It's Tiger Woods here."

OK, good one, buddy. He had a friend who could imitate Tiger to a tee, so he assumed it was the friend pulling his leg. The phone rang again. It was late, and Williams wasn't in the mood. He hung up a second time. But then a third call arrived, and Tiger had to blurt and plead, "No, it really is Tiger. I've just parted ways with my caddie and I want to know if you'd like to come caddie for me."

Williams said he'd think about it, and the following Monday he drove from Miami to Woods' home in Orlando to talk about it in person. Woods opened the door but quickly moved on to something else. "Come in, but can you wait a minute? I've got something I need to finish." He followed him inside to discover the thing he needed to finish was a video game.

"I had no concept of what he was trying to achieve in this game or even how to play the thing but could see how competitive he was," Williams recalled. "He was so focused on what was in front of him he was almost in a trance." He had been around golf enough to know the "look" the best golfers had. Floyd had the look. But this was a different level of focus and intensity, and it was over a video game. "I knew right then that he was different."

They talked and got to know each other, Williams explaining his caddying philosophies and how he values his abilities both as a strategist and as someone who understands the mind of a golfer. Williams was also a muscular, athletic former rugby player who loved to work out. Woods is somebody who often wouldn't trust people until he learned they were good golfers. He gains respect for people that way, and being a fitness fanatic is no different. They went on to work out together over time.

Woods hired him right then. The only request Williams made was he insisted on going home to New Zealand during off stretches. Tiger agreed. Suddenly Woods' entire career—and life—was changing. In the two years leading up to the 1999 PGA Championship win and his 2000 breakout, he developed the core of who he'd be for his peak. He had a new girlfriend, Joanna Jagoda. He had parted ways with long-time agent Hughes Norton, in part because Woods decided he wanted fewer commitments as he focused on golf, so he brought in IMG's Mark Steinberg, who became known as "Dr. No" for protecting Woods' time. Earl was around dramatically less, too. Woods had a brand-new swing developed with Harmon. And then he had a new caddie.

"I knew from the way he was playing this video game it was going to be a whole new kettle of fish," Williams said. "Tiger, even then, with one major to his name, was a world figure—not exclusively a golfing figure—and I knew I was going to have to give up my nice, easy lifestyle."

———

After the Memorial, Woods won the Western Open and finished T7 at the Open Championship at Carnoustie. He arrived at the 1999 PGA Championship at Medinah—at the time the longest course in major championship history—still as a man with just one career major victory. And he found himself in a Sunday duel with Sergio García, a nineteen-year-old Spanish rookie with plenty of hype behind him. García was brash and exciting, but he was also known for having a bad attitude. Kultida famously referred to him as "crybaby" often, and this matchup felt like the beginning of a nascent rivalry.

In the final round, Woods had a five-stroke lead with seven holes to go when García got hot in the group ahead of him. García went to the par 3 13th hole, a challenging hole to land the green let alone birdie, and sunk a lengthy putt to get within 3 while Woods and caddie Steve Williams watched from the 13th tee behind them. It wasn't the putt that caused a stir, though. It was the reaction, García spinning around to clench his right fist in the air while looking up and staring across the hole at Woods with a face as if to throw down the gauntlet.

"Did you see that?" Williams asked.

"Yes, I did," Woods said solemnly.

But unlike how the history books tend to remember Woods in these moments, it was the rare time it seemed to affect him adversely. Woods duffed a chip and double bogeyed 13 to drop the lead to one, a three-shot swing on one hole. "But it also galvanized his competitive resolve," Williams said. García, by then trailing by two on the 16, hit a miraculous shot from the tree line and sprinted up the fairway, scissor-kicking into the air as the crowd roared and the ball found the green. García somehow saved par, and another Woods' bogey on 16 kept the lead at one. He was letting García back in.

Then another mistake. Woods missed the green on the par 3 17th hole and needed a delicate, impressive chip on the slippery greens to get within six feet. The pressure was on, and for one of the first times in their new relationship, Woods trusted Williams to help with the read. Williams told him, "Inside left," and Woods said, "Perfect." He sunk the putt and gave Williams a quick wink. One hole later, he won the PGA Championship by one shot thanks to another par on 18. This wasn't Tiger Woods running away by 12 or coming up with the vicious, killer shots on Sunday. This was an escape.

"Tiger's first reaction was one of absolute relief—he was mentally exhausted," Williams wrote. "It had taken him more than two years to add a second major to his dominant maiden triumph at Augusta in 1997, and he'd had to fight for every single shot." But as the years have gone by, Williams looks back on that escape as a good thing. "The 1999 PGA Championship changed something in Tiger, lifted a weight of expectation. Gaining that elusive second major freed something in him and he accelerated his game to go on a peerless winning run."

Tiger 2.0 was unlocked from then on. He won four more tournaments in a row to wrap up 1999, including the Tour Championship. It gave him eight PGA Tour wins in the year, just the tenth golfer to ever achieve the feat. This was already one of the best seasons in golf history, but what would come next makes it seem so forgettable in hindsight. He opened 2000 by winning the Mercedes Championship in Hawaii and the AT&T Pebble Beach Pro-Am (where the US Open would be held later that year). That win in Pebble Beach came despite trailing by seven strokes and ultimately beating Vijay Singh and Matt Gogel by two. It was six consecutive tournament victories, the longest streak since Byron Nelson's eleven-tournament streak in 1945. Then, he finished 5th at the 2000 Masters because of a poor first round 75. He was livid with himself. He went to the Memorial, a course Woods said was set up in major-like conditions similar to the US Open, and won playing shots he imagined for Pebble Beach, not Muirfield. Everything, even the high-profile PGA Tour events that meant so much to most pros, was about preparing for majors.

"People said he was long but too wild, and he's become the best driver in the game," Harmon told a reporter in spring 2000. "They said he couldn't control his short irons because he swung too hard, said his wedge play wasn't any good. Now they're the strengths of his game because Tiger has worked. He hit 71 percent of his fairways last year; he led the Tour in hitting greens in regulation. He has got to putt more consistently, but when he putts well, he's phenomenal. He's a work in progress. Anything that's a weakness, he turns into a strength."

Shortly before the US Open, Woods and rising young Australian star Adam Scott played a practice round at Harmon's facility in Las Vegas. There were howling 35 mph winds, quite similar to the conditions they'd face the next week in Pebble Beach along the coast. Woods shot a 62 that came in spite of a penalty from an unplayable lie. Scott shot a 72. Scott walked back in saying, "Man, I've got a lot of work to do if I'm ever going to be this good."

Harmon had a different takeaway.

"We all rushed to the casino and made a bet on Tiger Woods to win the US Open."

———

Chapter Three

THE GAME WITHIN
THE GAME

Tiger Woods is the main character of this book, but Jack Nicklaus is the man hovering over each and every moment. He was the great one, the golden bear, the sports' preeminent champion with those eighteen majors and seventeen second-place major finishes. The way each great NBA player now has to combat the legend of Michael Jordan, anything and everything Woods accomplished was analyzed in direct comparison to what Nicklaus had done. And in 2000, in particular, parallels of Woods and Nicklaus would not go away. It was the year

Nicklaus played his final US Open and PGA Championship, bringing even more attention to the 100th US Open
at one of golf's great theaters, Pebble Beach.

Nicklaus was sixty. He had an artificial hip and
hadn't finished better than 27th in the US Open since
1986, although he did have an incredible 6th-place finish
at the 1998 Masters at fifty-eight. But the day before the
US Open, he was the story. The *Los Angeles Times* piece
from that Wednesday ended with a passing of the torch
to Woods, but of course with the caveats that Woods
only had two majors by twenty-four while Nicklaus had
four.

They'd never played a round together in a tournament,
but they knew each other well. Back in 1991, as Woods
was a fifteen-year-old junior gaining attention, Woods
went to Bel-Air Country Club to watch Nicklaus put on
a clinic. He was already being labeled a future star before
he won the first of three U.S. Juniors or broke Nicklaus'
U.S. Amateur records. Bel-Air represented a different
world for Tiger. He grew up just forty miles away, but this
club was the home of presidents and movie stars. A Black
member hadn't been invited until just a few years before.

Nicklaus invited the young Woods to come show his
swing. The entire crowd homed in on him as Woods hit

several balls and Nicklaus joked, "Tiger, when I grow up, I want to have a swing as pretty as yours." They spoke over the years as Woods rose through the ranks. Earlier in that year, Woods told a reporter, "We have an understanding of each other, just because of the way we play. The passion and the competitive drive we both have, it's inherent. I definitely sense something when I'm around him. We're a lot alike."

And at this point in time, Nicklaus was always happy to discuss how impressive Woods was. He raved about his talent and the ways he could become better than him. But those praises seemingly always came with slight comments that ensured the masses knew his accomplishments were still better.

"When I won majors, there were guys who had won majors themselves," Nicklaus said. "And that's the reason I probably got beat several times by [Tom] Watson or [Lee] Trevino or somebody else, because they knew how to win majors, which made it harder to win . . .

"Right now, we don't have many guys that have won majors that are playing. It's been all spread out. If Tiger is coming down to the end of a tournament, it's a lot easier for him to win that than somebody who hasn't won, versus what I had in competition."

The other element hanging over the 100th US Open was the loss of revered golfer Payne Stewart. Stewart was something of Woods' mentorship grandfather. Stewart took a young Mark O'Meara under his wing and taught him the ways of life on tour, and it was O'Meara who then mentored Woods throughout his rise. The three of them were neighbors at the Isleworth Golf and Country Club outside of Orlando, and all three were having a major moment in golf at the same time. O'Meara came out of seemingly nowhere to win two majors in 1998. Then Stewart won his third major championship at the 1999 US Open at Pinehurst, and Woods was of course the biggest star in the game and won his second major at the 1999 PGA Championship. That summer they went on a fishing trip together in Ireland and Stewart hit a hole-in-one at Ballybunion.

Three months later, Stewart died in a plane crash while flying to the Tour Championship on October 25, 1999, along with the five other people on board: pilots Michael Kling and Stephanie Bellegarrigue; his agent Robert Fraley; golf architect Bruce Borland; and the president of Leader Enterprises sports management agency, Van Ardan.

Since Stewart was the reigning US Open champ, the

week was filled with events honoring his legacy. One of those events was a 7 a.m. memorial on Pebble Beach's 18th green the day before the tournament. More than forty golfers lined up along Carmel Bay and did an homage to the twenty-one-gun salute, with a "Ready, aim, fire!" command spawning each golfer to launch balls into the water at sunrise. It was an emotional scene with widow Tracey Stewart in tears. Golfers like Paul Azinger, Phil Mickelson, Davis Love III, David Duval, Tom Lehman, Lee Janzen, and Sergio García were in attendance.

Tiger Woods was not, and that caused a stir.

Woods had a practice round scheduled at 7 a.m., and he felt he'd properly honored Stewart over the last few months and grieved with Tracey in private. He didn't think a public showing for the cameras was a necessary reason to limit his preparation for a US Open. While some golfers and reporters were getting worked up by the absence, Woods was off practicing for hours in a round with O'Meara. Then he spent more time on the practice greens making subtle adjustments when his putting didn't feel right. Celebrities tried to say hello, but Woods gave them no time. He was in no mood for anything distracting him from winning his third major championship.

Even when reporters hounded him about missing the ceremony, he didn't give in. In his mind, O'Meara knew Stewart longer and better than most, and he felt the same way about practicing instead. Jack Nicklaus wasn't there either. "It all depends on how you are personally," Woods said. "If that's how you want to put closure to it, that's how you put closure to it. I handle things a little differently . . . I loved the guy. But I've got to focus on what I've got to focus on, and I've already honored Payne. I thought [going] would be detrimental to my game this week."

The week was filled with discussions about things other than golf. For many, those types of moments were far more important than the game. Maybe in this later phase of his life, Woods would have felt the same. But not that year. Not that week. He spent eleven hours at the course that day grinding on his game to the point where Harmon watched and felt assured that nobody could hang with Woods. He watched Woods hit four perfect drives onto the difficult second fairway and was convinced he'd never seen Woods look more comfortable. "God, this is about as good as I've ever seen him swing," Harmon said to Williams on the tee box. "This is going to be a fun week."

Paul Goydos was in that practice group, too. The

thirty-five-year-old tour pro couldn't believe what he saw, Woods hitting countless different shots with the same club that most players didn't have in their bag at all. He could go farther. He could fly it higher. Goydos walked off the 18th green when a fan asked about Woods.

"This tournament is over," Goydos replied. "He's going to win by ten shots."

Johnny Miller, the 1973 US Open champ and longtime NBC golf analyst, watched him that Wednesday and felt an aura around Woods. So much so that he made his own proclamation on the broadcast. He turned to play-by-play man Dan Hicks and said, "I think he's going to win by a record score and just run away with this thing." Hicks stared at him in confusion. That was a *strong* take as a tournament just began.

The greatest year in golf had been bubbling. Now, it was going to truly begin.

———

Woods opened with a first round 65. It helped that he got the good side of the draw with an early morning tee time while the conditions got more challenging as the day went on. He jumped out to a solo first-round lead with Miguel Ángel Jiménez just behind him at 5-under par.

As Harmon said, the difference in whether Woods would run away with a major or whether it would be a tight contest came down to his putter. The rest always seemed to be steady. As he worked with Harmon for eleven hours that Wednesday before the tournament, two and a half of those hours were spent on the putting green. Something didn't feel right. They made little adjustments to his posture. They fixed his release, too.

That week, he didn't three-putt once. He made his first putt on 20 of 38 holes. It was putting perfection on some of the trickiest, bumpiest greens in the world.

"He had some jedi powers. He could pretty much will the ball in the hole," said Jesper Parnevik, who played the first two rounds that week with Woods. "And sometimes I could swear he did because I would think the ball was going to miss or already had missed, and it would go in sideways. That's some strong-ass, Obi-Wan Kenobi jedi stuff going on."

But greatness in golf is rarely about how well you play when the conditions are good. The most ingrained memories aren't the low-scoring birdie fests. They are when the test becomes so challenging that the field withers away, yet the protagonist maintains.

Friday, the windy, foggy conditions along the California coastline made the difficult setup at Pebble Beach seemingly impossible. A fog delay set start times back a few hours. Nicklaus finished his final US Open round as he failed to make the cut. And Woods didn't tee off until 4:40 p.m. He only played 12 holes by the time the round was called for darkness, but he played those 12 holes in 3-under par, including a now famous shot on Pebble's famous par-5 sixth hole. Woods found himself in the rough and behind the tall Monterey pine trees for his second shot, one that requires golfers to hit up onto a large cliff to reach in two. Analyst Roger Maltbie recalled plenty of players hitting into that rough on 6, and all had to lay up to the hill. "Nobody could contemplate what Tiger did with that shot," Maltbie said. "You couldn't picture it, you couldn't imagine it."

Woods admitted later that, sure, he thought he could catch a flier if he came down steep enough on the ball to get it to the top of the hill, but even he didn't think he'd reach the green. He crushed a 7-iron so hard he had to lean sideways to not fall over. It made its way over the pines and flew 205 yards over the trees and up the hill to the green for a two-putt birdie. Williams shook his head in disbelief. Woods looked like he was playing another sport that day. He's played better tournaments from tee to green, but he couldn't miss a putt on Pebble's notoriously bumpy Poa greens. By the time he finished round two Saturday morning, second place was down to 2-under par. Woods was 8-under.

———

What happened the next morning we know. The lost golf balls. The stressful finish with a ball in the water. Those were all details we didn't learn until much later. All we knew was he had a six-shot lead at the US Open.

The actual story of the morning at the time showed the other side of how Woods was covered. He was the biggest star in sports. Period. Jordan had retired. All eyes were on Woods, especially at a major, and the world wasn't quite ready to see its perfect chosen one unleashing expletives on national TV early in the morning. He lived with a different standard as a prodigy. His father proclaimed he'd bring peace to the world. So, when he yelled, "Goddamn you fucking prick!" among other things after his 18th tee shot went into the water, it jarred many audience members.

Viewers called NBC to complain, and NBC sent reporter Jimmy Roberts to interview Woods after the round and ask him about the cursing. Roberts didn't want to blindside Woods, so he went up to Woods and Jagoda and warned them that he had to ask about it. Woods wasn't exactly appreciative.

Golfers get angry on the course. It's common. Two-time major winner Jon Rahm got constant criticism early in his career for his outbursts, and his reputation changed less so when he stopped getting angry but when broadcasts stopped harping on it. Scheffler, the current world No. 1, gets livid on golf courses, shouting and throwing balls into the trees out of frustration. And Woods was no different. He was an extreme competitor, so of course he let out his emotions. But there was a disconnect in how Woods was portrayed and who he was. Meaning he was human. He had feelings, like any other golfer. But his image was some type of purity-based robot.

Roberts made his case that it was simply a chance to explain and apologize. Jagoda convinced Woods that Roberts was right, and Roberts asked him about the incident.

"Yeah, I got a little angry," Woods said. "I kinda let the emotions get the better of myself. I hit a bad shot. I was trying to hit a nice little straight ball out there, and I hit a pull hook. And I guess I got a little upset. I'm sorry I did get upset, but I think anyone in that situation would get a little perturbed at themselves. Unfortunately, I let it voice out loud."

It looked like a normal interview and Woods handled it well. What Roberts didn't know immediately was right then he got on Woods' bad side.

———

The way Tiger was playing, the tournament was likely over by Saturday morning, but he gave the field a brief moment of hope in the third round when a gust of wind took his ball and left it in some thick greenside rough. He could barely see the ball and could hardly hit it either, but he didn't want to take a drop. He tried to hit it sideways and take the loss, but it didn't move more than a yard. He tried this time to go for the green, but it fell well short. At best, he was going to double bogey, but he missed the eight-foot putt to triple bogey to drop from 9-under to 6-under.

The problem was nobody else finished the round under par.

Even after the triple bogey, he led Ernie Els by 10 shots through 54 holes. He was the only golfer in the field under par, and he was *8* shots under. For most of us, that is when we go into autopilot. But that is not how it works inside the mind of Tiger Woods. He entered Sunday with a new mission.

He approached the first tee wearing a dark, blood-red Nike golf shirt. His signature. He says he wears red because of Kultida. "My mom thought, being a Capricorn, that [red] was my power color," he said. But a young Tiger, like most teenagers, was stubborn and wore blue to spite her. He did not win those tournaments.

"So, Mom is always right," he joked.

Els, playing with him Sunday, thought the weather might give him a chance. He even thought he played well from tee to green. But Ernie Els did not stand a chance.

Woods approached Pebble Beach's famous 7th hole, a beautiful short par 3 with the water and a cliff along the right side. The normal etiquette for No. 7 is to hit your ball onto the green, mark your ball, and step off to allow the group ahead on No. 8 to tee off. In the final round, Pádraig Harrington and Miguel Ángel Jiménez were in the group in front.

Well, there must have been some sort of delay, because Woods didn't feel like waiting. Williams looked up and saw Woods preparing to putt before Harrington and Jiménez teed off.

"Are you going to wait for them?" Williams asked.

"No," Woods said. "I'm going to make them stand there and watch me bury this putt."

There's an old story about Michael Jordan that has become folklore. It goes that a relative no-name Washington Bullet named LaBradford Smith scored his lone career 30-point game when dropping 37 on Jordan's Bulls in 1993 while Jordan shot 9-of-27. Jordan claimed that after the game, Smith went up to Jordan and dismissively said, "Nice game, Mike." It set Jordan off. He took this seemingly innocuous comment and used it as fuel, telling teammates he'd drop Smith's 37 in the first half alone against them the next night. By the way, the Bulls *won* that first game anyway. But Jordan didn't think like normal people. He was so incredibly dominant that he needed to find these little missions to keep himself motivated. Jordan scored 36 that first half and 47 for the game in a Bulls win while homing in on Smith. Smith never scored more than 19 points in a single game the rest of his career, and he was out of the league by summer 1994. Years later, Jordan was asked if Smith actually even said, "Nice game, Mike." He said no. He made it up.

Woods was wired similarly. He often said golf is a game in which you need "mini goals" each day. Before the 2019 Presidents Cup, a little-known Mexican golfer named Abraham Ancer was asked who he'd like to face in Sunday singles. Ancer, a then-twenty-eight-year-old who grew up idolizing Woods, said he'd like to face Tiger. Woods didn't interpret it like most of us, as Ancer saying playing Woods would be a dream. So, when he did in fact face Ancer in Sunday singles and beat him, Woods cockily said, "Abe wanted it. He got it."

If you didn't know this about him, you would have been confused on the 16th hole on Sunday at Pebble Beach—with an astronomical lead and three holes to go—as Woods sunk a lengthy par putt and launched into an emotional fist pump. He did his iconic Woods strut and appeared locked in like it was a playoff. Why? He was 4-under for the day without a single bogey. That created a new mission.

As he walked to the 16th green, he told Williams, "I don't care what you say. I don't care what you do. I am not making a bogey today, Steve." On television later that night, he said, "If I missed that putt I would have been ticked at myself. To be honest with you, I never thought of any records. All I wanna do is make no bogeys."

Woods was in his own little world. He was now in a battle with himself. His game for the day was to ensure he played a seemingly mistake-free round without a single lost stroke. Winning the US Open wouldn't be enough. In order to actually feel like he achieved something, he'd need to finish the final hurdle.

The evil irony of 18 that day was that Woods did not hit to driver, as Williams wished he would the day before. He hit a 4-iron to the center of the fairway. No bogeys. Then, instead of going for the green, he laid up with a 7-iron. No bogeys. He approached his ball to the sounds of Pebble Beach crowning him as the champion golfer in the United States. Woods placed his wedge shot safely on the green, and Woods and Williams gave each other a fist bump. Well, they tried to. It was one of those situations where one guy expects a high five and the other expects a fist. They awkwardly nearly missed, Woods bumping Williams' wrist instead.

Woods missed his birdie putt four feet past the hole. To achieve his goal, he had to actually focus on this final par putt with a 15-shot lead. He took his time, read the situation, and made it.

He ran off and hugged Kultida. Earl Woods was not there, but NBC's Roberts asked if he had a message for him.

"Not too bad of a Father's Day present," Woods said.

Second place at the 2000 US Open was 3-over par, tied between Els and Jiménez. A prestigious top 10 major finish could be earned with a mere 7-over. Woods finished at 12-*under* par. He let out a cheesy, kid-like smile and a fist pump as the final putt went in. It was the first time in history a golfer finished a US Open at double digits under par. Shoot, it was only the second time a player had *reached* 10-under at a US Open. His 15-shot victory passed the 138-year major record held by Old Tom Morris' 13-shot win at the 1862 Open Championship. And when it was over, Johnny Miller proclaimed it the greatest four rounds of golf ever played. Few have argued in the twenty-five years since.

"I don't know how much more there is to say about him," Els said after the round. "We've talked about him for two years now, and I guess we're going to talk about him for the next three.

"He just played a perfect US Open week. He did nothing wrong."

The numbers support it. In the advanced statistic "strokes gained: total," which measures how many shots a golfer gains on the field each round, Woods compiled 29.2 total strokes gained on the field that week. Per statistician Justin Ray, it's the highest total of any US Open in the modern era. But that's not the jarring part. The gap between Woods' 2000 US Open and the second best US Open performance ever is 3.91 strokes gained. That's the same distance between No. 2 and No. 19 on the list. He had the best scoring average on every type of hole: par 3s, par 4s, and par 5s. Of the 437 rounds played that week, only three didn't have a bogey. Two of those were by Woods. He was playing a different sport.

So as Els and Jiménez stood and watched on the side of the 18th green, Woods celebrated and earned his applause. Jiménez, tied with Els for second place, turned to a tournament official.

"Excuse me, can you tell me when the playoff starts for the other tournament between me and Ernie?"

Chapter Four

THE TWO SLAMS

Tiger Woods had just whipped him in a friendly game back at Isleworth a few days before. It was the final sign to O'Meara that this kid was ready. The two hopped on a shared private flight to Augusta for the 1997 Masters. Woods hadn't even played in a major as a professional. He was twenty-one. He was the favorite to win. He didn't know what he didn't know, and maybe that made him all the more powerful.

He asked O'Meara a question.

"Do you think it's possible to win the Grand Slam?"

O'Meara took a moment, likely considering all the legends who failed to come close to the feat. "Unrealistic," he said. Woods wasn't as sure, but he kept quiet. They flew on to Augusta, where Woods would run away with his first green jacket. He wouldn't win another major for more than two years, but even then the greatest heights were on his mind.

Golf's Grand Slam occupies a foreign place in sporting lore, the pantheon achievement that toes this perfectly enticing line of unattainable yet possible. It is like Ted Williams being the last baseball player to hit .400 multiplied by 10, perhaps the most sought-after and glorified seasonal achievement in all of sports. And the mystique only grows with the fact that it has simultaneously never been achieved *and* achieved twice, depending on your definition. It is argued over and debated in terms of what officially qualifies. And it's in that gap that golfers will forever yearn for that slight possibility of reaching a new summit.

Most golfers growing up were taught that Bobby Jones is the only golfer to win a Grand Slam, which he did in 1930 to reach thirteen career major championships, the record Nicklaus ultimately broke. Jones is something of golf's Babe Ruth, the patriarchal legendary figure that all American golf stems from, or at least that's how it's chronicled. He was the best of his era while only playing as an amateur, and then after his retirement he designed Augusta National with Alister MacKenzie for what became the host site of the Masters and the most famous course in golf.

And yes, Jones did it. In 1930, he won the US Open, the Open Championship, the U.S. Amateur, and the British Amateur, which were then the agreed-upon four majors. Nobody had ever done it before, so the scribes of the time battled to find ways to encapsulate the absurdity of Jones' year. George Trevor of the *New York Sun* wrote: "Atlanta's first citizen, like Napoleon before him, has stormed the supposedly impregnable 'quadrilateral.' Bob is the first golfer in all history to win the four major championships—American open, American amateur, British open and finally the British amateur." It was then *Atlanta Journal* writer O. B. Keeler who dubbed it the "Grand Slam" in 1930. That title stuck more than "quadrilateral."

But the cynics or modernists will be quick to say that Jones was competing for a completely different Grand Slam. Two of them were amateur events, which were certainly agreed to be some of the biggest tournaments but meant Jones wasn't competing against top pros. Jones can't be punished for the Masters not existing yet, especially since he created it, but he also didn't compete in the PGA Championship because he remained an amateur and was not a professional.

This modern version of what we call the four legs of the Grand Slam took time. The Masters was founded in 1934, but even then nobody had quite proclaimed it a "major." As much as it feels like ancient law now, the term "major" is an arbitrary declaration the golf world decided on retroactively. Usually by writers. The PGA Tour didn't exist until the 1970s. Professional golf remained a scattered, practically unconnected series of tournaments with no established format or agreed-upon regulations. Still, the Masters was immediately a premier event, and the closest anyone came before Woods to achieving the slam was Ben Hogan in 1953. And even that comes with its own frustrating asterisk.

Hogan won the Masters and the US Open, but the PGA Championship overlapped with the British Open. At this point, the concept of the modern four *professional* majors still hadn't been formed, so maybe the tournament organizers can be forgiven for not preventing overlap. The PGA was not considered a major—it had a match play format until switching to stroke play in 1958—so Hogan normally went overseas instead and, of course, won the

Open at Carnoustie by four shots. He won all three "majors" he played in 1953, but we'll never know if he would have pulled off all four.

The first notion of the modern professional Grand Slam didn't start until *Pittsburgh Press* writer Bob Drum, one of golf's great scribes, suggested it in print after Arnold Palmer's 1960 Masters win. Drum wrote that if Palmer followed up his Masters win with victories at the US Open, the Open Championship, and the PGA Championship, it might match Jones' famous 1930 Grand Slam. But the more well-known part of the story came when Drum accompanied Palmer on the transatlantic flight to the Open at St Andrews that summer. He pitched Palmer on his idea.

"One thing led to another," Palmer said. "Drum got me all excited about it. He wrote about it. He got the British press all excited about it. And they picked up on it."

It gained steam, but it remained common for there to be scheduling issues between the Open and the PGA. Five times in the 1960s the two were held in consecutive weeks, which still made it difficult for most to pull off playing both (plus, nobody was coming close to winning them all anyway). It wasn't until the Tournament Players Division formed in 1968, and later became what's now the PGA Tour, that a larger governing body attempted to regulate things like schedules. And even now, the PGA Tour doesn't actually own any of the majors. They are all individual entities that can do whatever they want. Still, the PGA Championship finally moved to August in 1969, where it stayed until moving to May in 2019.

Even before the solidification of these four as the new marquee, Palmer and Nicklaus played in all four each year going back to 1960 as their primes intertwined. Neither ever won more than two in a year. Both only won two in a row once. Palmer won the Masters and US Open in 1960, and Nicklaus did the same in 1972.

When Nicklaus won that US Open in 1972, it carried all the parallels to what followed Woods in 2000. From the moment Nicklaus earned his fourth green jacket at the 1972 Masters, every conversation revolved around whether the best in the world could accomplish his pursuit. It was even more fitting that the 1972 US Open was the first major ever played at a daunting Pebble Beach, and again the conditions were so brutal that nobody finished under par. Legendary *Sports Illustrated* golf writer Dan Jenkins, something of golf's great ombudsman throughout its rise in popularity, wrote: "Jack Nicklaus kept a personal rendezvous by winning the prettiest—and in some ways the most important—US Open

Championship ever played. On the toughest course there ever was, he beat the best there are."

So much of the story of the week was the way Pebble destroyed golfer after golfer to put up scores representing the early 1900s, and Jenkins wrote that history shouldn't focus on the scores but the way Nicklaus performed against such a test: "that it should be stated here and now that under the circumstances it was as brilliant as any man ever shot." The entire tournament was covered in a way that made it about Nicklaus vs. Bobby Jones, not Nicklaus vs. the field. When he finally took the trophy, Arnold Palmer said of his longtime rival, "From now on, he's going to have trouble even breathing."

And exactly like Woods at the upcoming 2000 Open Championship at St Andrews, Nicklaus entered the 1972 Open at Muirfield as an identical 2-to-1 betting favorite. The *Scotsman* newspaper labeled its daily coverage "The Grand Slam Open," with a large photo of Nicklaus. And when his nearly miraculous late run fell short to the great Lee Trevino, the story was hardly about how Trevino won it. It was about how Nicklaus *lost* it, coming in with far too conservative a game plan while the course played easier than expected, how he waited too long to begin attacking. In that final round, his putts simply didn't fall, and Nicklaus finished second. A month later, he finished T13 at the PGA Championship, cementing another campaign for the slam that fell just short.

It is a reminder of how, even against greats of the game like Trevino, Palmer, Gary Player, Tony Jacklin, and so on, Nicklaus was written about like he was supposed to win— that he entered major season as the man chasing history, not just a great player hoping to win. It was a pressure that perhaps only Woods can relate to. And despite how dominant Nicklaus may have been, not even he could win more than two majors in a row.

Jenkins wrote that day in Muirfield: "He can keep trying for the Grand Slam, which might only exist in a dream, after all."

Perhaps for greater context on how impossible the season Grand Slam is, just know the "career Grand Slam" remains the most exclusive club in the game. To this day, only five golfers have ever won all four of the modern majors. Gene Sarazen was the first, winning seven career majors, but that was somewhat retroactive since it was before the PGA and Masters were proclaimed majors. Hogan won them all as well, finishing off the quadrilateral at the 1953 Open, where he won his third major of the season. Next was the South African great Gary Player with his nine career majors, beating Nicklaus to it by winning the 1965 US Open before Nicklaus could finally win a British Open. A year later, Nicklaus joined the list with his 1966 Open Championship win at Muirfield, the same place that robbed him of his season Grand Slam in 1972.

Nobody else joined the club for thirty-five years. Palmer never won a PGA Championship. Neither did Tom Watson with his eight majors. Walter Hagen's prime was before the Masters, and his best finish at Augusta was T11 when the tournament did finally begin. Sam Snead and Phil Mickelson both failed to ever win a US Open. Trevino never won a Masters, although that was mainly because he only played it twice due to feuds with Augusta management. McIlroy and Spieth both won three of the four by their early twenties, yet as of publication, McIlroy hasn't won a Masters despite constant close calls, and Spieth hasn't won a PGA Championship.

And in July 2000, Woods had three of four as he made his way to St Andrews. He'd finished third in 1998 thanks to a final round 66 to finish one off the playoff that his old buddy O'Meara won. In 1999, he finished T7. Before anybody was seriously talking about "Tiger Slams" or winning four majors in a row, Woods needed to finally earn the career slam. And it had to happen overseas.

———

Chapter Five

THE MARKET MOVER

Why?

T he advertisement spread across a double truck presentation in newspapers and magazines around the
world asking the simplest question. It did not use his
name. It did not spell anything else out. The ad was almost entirely white space aside from a few sentences of
spread-out text and one singular golf ball sitting up on
grass.

It listed every major accomplishment in Woods' short

yet dominant career. From the USGA junior championships to the collegiate national titles to the three majors
to the seventeen career wins. It asked a simple question.
Why would a man who's won all those accolades decide
to change his ball? The ad, quite brilliantly, answered the
question: "Because he's only won . . ." all those tournaments. It should be even more, it suggested.

That was it. That was the advertisement for the Nike
Tour Accuracy golf ball in 2000 that changed the golf
equipment game from there on out. And to make this
seismic shift, there was just one person who could truly
move the needle. One person whose use and endorsement
on the largest stages would sway the greater golfing world.
And that person didn't need to be named. Anybody even
remotely following sports in 2000 knew the ad was about
Tiger Woods.

That move was happening in secret over the previous
eighteen months, the perfectionist Woods constantly testing and adjusting to create the ball that would be *his*, the
one that would help elevate him not just from the most
talented golfer but to the greatest of his era.

At this point, Woods had a long relationship with
Titleist since turning pro in 1996 and used the Titleist
Professional ball. Balls in those days were primarily

made of balata, a rubberlike substance culled from trees in Central and South America. They had a liquid core inside with rubber bands wrapped around it. Those balata balls often scuffed within a few holes and tour pros tossed balls out and might use just three balls across nine holes. Woods, though, used the Titleist Professional, an adjustment that used an elastomer cover around the liquid core to better withstand faster impact speeds (like Woods').

Nike was not a player in the golf equipment game. Not yet it wasn't. Yes, it had a historic twenty-year, $40 million deal with Woods since he turned pro, creating iconic ads that only added to Woods' legend, like the "Hello world" ad on the day he turned pro, but the deal was for apparel and shoes. Nike was an outfitter. In fact, Titleist's parent company, Acushnet Company, sued Nike in 1999 in the US District court in Boston after they claimed two Nike commercials—including an iconic video of Woods bouncing a golf ball on his club like he was playing hacky sack—used deceptive advertising by insinuating Woods was using Nike equipment in ads that ended with a big Nike logo. Nike denied any deceptive advertising, and Titleist later renegotiated its deal with Woods as it settled with Nike.

But Nike was, in fact, on a mission to capitalize on

the booming golf industry that Woods was certainly helping to popularize, so they got to work with Japan-based
manufacturer Bridgestone to create a new ball. Hideyuki
"Rock" Ishii was the mastermind engineer behind it all. He
and Nike global director of sports marketing Pat Devlin
waited on Woods' every beck and call, flying across the
world with prototypes in suitcases to test with Woods to
build a ball perfect for his specifications. The focus of Ishii's
new masterpiece was a different type of material, a three-
piece ball with a molded rubber core injected with synthetic
material, and a multilayer urethane cover. Its goal was to
offer a similar feel but with less spin and more speed.

As far back as January 1999, Woods worked with Ishii
and Devlin, prototyping constantly before the last test in
March 2000 in Newport Beach, California. They loved
testing with him because of his innate feel for each little
detail. Stories have been told about Woods being able to
notice the most minuscule changes in weights between
drivers just from holding them, and with ball testing he
noticed the tiniest difference in sound when the ball hit
his putter. He was happy with this ball, though. It added
10 mph of velo, and he loved the way it flew through the
wind. But that March Woods told them he wanted one
more test before he put it in play. He didn't want to rush it,

so that final test would have to wait until after the major season.

That was until Woods sat in frustration in May following a close defeat at the Byron Nelson Classic. Devlin sent Woods a text message telling Woods he played well. This was a month before Woods' dominant US Open and weeks before his 2000 campaign truly took off. He'd already won three times in 2000, reclaiming his place as world No. 1, but he could see the missing piece. Twenty minutes after getting the text message, Woods called Devlin at his home in Portland, where he put the glass of wine down to speak to the best player in the world.

"Can you meet me in Germany Tuesday morning?" Woods asked.

Devlin was confused and surprised. Sure, he could, but why? Woods told him he wanted to put the ball in play that week at the Deutsche Bank-SAP Open in Hamburg, Germany. Devlin, like Steve Williams in the hotel before him, did not believe Tiger Woods. And once again, Woods had to make himself clear.

"No, I'm serious," he said. "If I'd had my ball, I would have won by six."

The key was the phrase "my ball." That's what really made Devlin know this was for real. Suddenly Woods took ownership of their little project, and he was serious about taking it to the mainstream. And Tiger doing it was different. Nike launched its first set of golf balls in 1998, and it even had a PGA Tour winner use Nike balls in Glen Day in 1999. But none of the top guys were on board, and nobody moved a market like Woods.

Woods asked him to bring five dozen balls to Germany. That was a challenge. It sparked a chaotic series of hours trying to get the balls from Japan to Germany on such short notice with a series of phone calls between Devlin, Ishii, Sternberg, and Nike Golf president Bob Wood. Within twenty minutes of Devlin's call to Ishii, Rock was in the car speeding to the Bridgestone plant to fetch the balls and booking an early morning flight to Hamburg to meet Woods on the first tee for a Tuesday practice round.

When Devlin and Ishii arrived, they were met by Williams, who told them it might not be the best day for the test due to bad weather. Woods walked up moments later and put that concern to bed. He thought it was the perfect day to find out if this ball was the best, because he'd really see it in the conditions that make a difference. First, Woods drove the usual Titleist ball, and the left-to-right wind took it into a right-side bunker. Then he used the Nike ball and, according to people there, hit it on the exact same line. This time, the weather hardly affected it, and it landed on the left side of the fairway. By the end of that practice round, he was sure he was changing to the new Nike Tour Accuracy ball. Woods played well in Germany, and then he took the ball to the Memorial in Ohio, where he won by five shots, and where Nicklaus, sitting next to him at the winner's press conference, proclaimed, "When you have the ability to just outdistance your opponents by 30 or 40 yards and know exactly what you're doing and where it's going to go, you just—you're playing for second every week . . . unless he doesn't play well."

On June 1, 2000, two weeks before the US Open in Pebble Beach, where Woods would shatter records, Woods secretly hid backstage at Nike Golf's semiannual footwear and equipment sales meetings at the Sunriver Resort in Oregon. Not even Bob Wood, as he took the stage to discuss plans for the next six months, knew that Woods was there. Woods then appeared from behind a curtain carrying a large framed photo of himself holding the Memorial trophy and the Nike ball he used to win.

The audience went wild, and Wood used expletives in confusion at the surprise reveal.

"Before we get started," Woods said, "I just want to tell you and everyone here that I've decided to switch permanently to the Nike Tour Accuracy ball."

That spring at the 2000 Masters, fifty-nine of ninety-five players in the field were still using wound, liquid-core balls. By the 2001 Masters, all but four were using solid-core balls.

———

The beauty of a figure like Tiger Woods is he can create tall tales that spread like wildfire and leave us unsure of what's the truth. But eventually the legend gets printed enough that it becomes the truth, because the myth tells us more about the way Woods operated throughout the world than the facts do. And in this case, it tells us how badly the moneymakers really wanted to sign him.

That's how Earl Woods could tell reporters that the first time IMG and its superagent Hughes Norton reached out about courting Woods was when he was five years old. Tom Callahan, one of the preeminent chroniclers of Woods' life and journey, wrote in the book *His Father's Son: Earl and Tiger Woods* that Norton kept clippings of everything going on in the sports world, and Norton saw the clips of Woods on television as a boy and bolted to the Woods home to make the connection. The story goes that Norton spoke to Earl while Woods rode a tricycle out front.

Norton's version is a bicycle. And that Woods was thirteen, not five. He said he'd been tracking him for years and finally made the trip to Cypress to meet him in 1989 after Woods finished second at the Big "I" Insurance Classic, a huge junior event where thousands of kids aged thirteen to eighteen fight to qualify for 108 spots. Woods, just thirteen, finished second. The only person to beat him? An eighteen-year-old Justin Leonard. Making the cut meant juniors got to play the third round accompanied by a PGA Tour player. Woods was paired with a twenty-three-year-old John Daly, where Daly trailed the five-foot-five thirteen-year-old by three shots through nine holes. Sure, Daly got hot and ultimately won by one, but the legend of Woods was spreading.

Woods shook hands with Norton and showed him his room. They spoke for a few minutes, Norton noticing the clippings of Nicklaus' career accomplishments that Woods would spend his life chasing. He noticed the lack of trophies, because by eleven there were 113 of them, and Kultida made Woods throw most of them away. After a short talk, Woods took off on a *bicycle*, according to Norton, as the grown-ups kept discussing his future.

As Norton and Earl walked to the door, Earl said, "The first Black superstar in golf is going to make himself and someone else a whole lot of money."

"That's why I'm here, Mr. Woods," Norton said. "That's why I'm here."

Who knows which timeline is true, but the myth tells the greater story of how early Woods was sought after. Norton and IMG founder Mark McCormack spent years building that relationship with Earl, Kultida, and Tiger, to the point Norton came up with the idea for essentially paying Earl without paying him for the way-too-early amateur relationship. Money was tight for the family with all the constant travel for a teenage golf phenom, so Norton thought of creating the job of a junior golf talent scout. After getting approval from the USGA because of the fine line they were toeing, IMG was paying Earl Woods $25,000 plus expenses as early as 1992. Other reports said it was $50,000 a year. All agree they tried to keep the deal quiet to not raise any red flags in the meantime. Of course, Woods signed with Norton and IMG when he turned pro in 1996.

This was the beginning of creating a billionaire athlete who made millions for so many others in his orbit. From the moment Tiger turned pro, Nike paid him $6.5 million a year on top of a $7.5 million signing bonus, more than triple what Reebok paid Greg Norman. Titleist gave him $20 million over five years. He had secured $60 million in commitments before his first professional shot.

As his career developed, he became the undeniable most marketable man in sports. Jordan might have changed the way shoes and apparel were marketed forever, becoming a billionaire in his own right thanks to shoe sales long after his retirement, but Woods took it to another level. Over the course of his career, Nike paid him more than $500 million. Gatorade gave him a $100 million deal. Electronic Arts reportedly gave him north of $100 million as the face of its golf video games for sixteen years. General Motors, Accenture, Gillette, TAG Heuer, NetJets—practically every big brand gave Woods big dollars, at least until many bowed out following his 2009 infidelity scandal. All of this came on top of $150 million in earnings from tournament winnings. As of April 2024, *Forbes* estimated Woods has earned $1.8 billion.

"Everybody was looking for the next Michael, and

they were always looking on the basketball court," Nike chairman Phil Knight said in 2000. "He was walking down the fairway."

And all of golf rose on the Tiger tidal wave. It was already a sport growing in popularity, but the difference with Woods was exponential. PGA Tour executive Donna Orender said in 2000, "After he came on the scene, he turbo-charged our ratings." CBS claimed there was a 71 percent difference in viewership between tournaments Woods played in 1999 and tournaments he didn't. That meant more money flowing into the sport. In 1996, the PGA Tour handed out $101 million in prize money. In 2024, that was north of $400 million.

Go back to that conversation between Norton and Earl and understand the "why" in Woods' astronomical value. Yes, he was the greatest young phenom the sport had ever seen. Yes, he brought charisma and excitement to a sport that hasn't always had it. Yes, everyone wanted to watch this player do things nobody had ever done before. But golf was and is a niche sport that in a vacuum has never truly competed with professional football or basketball. Yet in February 2000, when Woods was going for his seventh straight win at the Buick Invitational, the ratings beat the NBA All-Star Game by 15 percent.

The reality is that much of Woods' popularity came from the way he broke down barriers. He was the first Black man to win a major and the first to become an international golf star. He opened up new markets. He brought the game to different audiences.

Another of the famous Nike "Hello world" ads aired right as Woods made his professional debut in 1996. Over a collage of images of Woods' youth and amateur careers, no words were spoken. Just music and printed words.

"Hello world," it began, cutting to one line after another listing the unprecedented rise of Woods, from shooting in the seventies by age eight and playing in the Nissan Open by sixteen. How he won a U.S. Amateur by eighteen and became the only man to win it three years in a row. But the punch of the ad came at the end. "There are still courses in the U.S. I am not allowed to play because of the color of my skin. Hello world. I've heard I'm not ready for you. Are you ready for me?"

When Nike first showed Woods the ad, he immediately asked to watch it again. On the second watch, Harmon shouted, "That's the best fuckin' ad I've ever seen."

It became one of the more famous ads in Nike history, but it also caused backlash. Golfers and golf writers wondered about the sensationalism of leaning into race. When a *Washington Post* columnist questioned Nike about there being courses Woods still couldn't play, Nike conceded there weren't any and it wasn't meant to be taken literally, but Woods has long maintained he dealt with incidents of racism on golf courses in his youth. Woods was just twenty, and he wasn't quite prepared for the constant questions about what the world supposedly wasn't ready for or what his feelings were on race. He usually brushed off the questions or said the ad made people think for themselves.

This is where Woods and race become so difficult to pin down. Throughout his career, he simultaneously steered away from being a crucial civil rights force and used it to his advantage when necessary. He was the son of Earl, a man who suffered through racism his entire life and idolized trailblazers like Joe Louis. Earl talked constantly of race, and from one interview after another he put those pressures on Tiger to "do more than any other man in history to change the course of humanity." He told *Sports Illustrated*'s Gary Smith that Tiger would do more for the world than Buddha, Gandhi, or Nelson Mandela because he had a larger forum.

Therein lied the projection of the father onto the son, yet the son never raised his hand for this challenge. Earl's father wanted Earl to be a professional baseball player.

He'd seen Jackie Robinson break the color barrier in 1947 and claimed that while working as a batboy in Griffith Park in Manhattan, Kansas, he caught for Satchel Paige during batting practice. He played ball at Kansas State and liked to claim he broke the Big 7 conference color barrier, something later proven untrue. But his experiences in those years formed him. One time, an opposing collegiate coach in Mississippi told Earl's coach that Earl would have to go back on the bus since a Black player couldn't play. Another time in Oklahoma, a motel manager wouldn't let Earl stay at the hotel with the team. He also claimed a racist colonel stopped him from rising up higher in the military ranks.

But Woods didn't want to talk about race. When his Stanford team was invited to play an event at Shoal Creek Club in Alabama, a course famous for denying Black members, some teammates and Earl talked about why he shouldn't play there. Woods brushed it off. When a *New York Times Magazine* reporter asked him if the club's racist background added incentive, he just said, "No." While Earl revered his hero Louis for speaking out on issues, Woods told a reporter, "The only time I think about race is when the media ask me."

And while Woods didn't identify as deeply as his father with racial issues, he leaned into them from time to time.

As far back as an interview at fourteen, Tiger said, "Every time I go to a major country club, you can always feel it, you can always sense it. People are always staring at you. 'What are you doing here? You shouldn't be here . . . Why are you here? You're not supposed to be here.'" And even at fourteen, he understood the way he represented a new frontier. "Since I'm black, it might be even bigger than Jack Nicklaus. I might be even bigger than him—to the blacks," he said. "I might be sort of like a Michael Jordan in basketball. Something like that."

Plus, Woods always paid immense respect to the Black golfers who paved the way for him. When he won the 1997 Masters, he spotted Lee Elder in the crowd. Elder was the first Black man to play in the Masters, and Woods stopped to hug Elder and say, "Thanks for making this possible." On the other hand, he skipped the Clinton invitation to honor Jackie Robinson breaking the color barrier fifty years before.

And whether he liked engaging with it or not, race followed him. While Woods was running away with that Masters, becoming the first Black major winner, former Masters champ Fuzzy Zoeller infamously tried to joke: "That little boy is driving well and he's putting well. He's doing everything it takes to win. So, you know what you guys do when he gets in here? You pat him on the back and say congratulations and enjoy it and tell him not to serve fried chicken next year. Got it. Or collard greens or whatever the hell they serve." Zoeller apologized for it, but then he spent the next few years complaining that people wouldn't let it go.

The problem for Woods was that people were ready to jump on anything he did that counteracted the sorts of messages that used race. Shortly after the Masters win—and the Zoeller incident—he sat down for an interview with Oprah Winfrey where he cried at messages read by his father. But he also said it bothered him to be referred to as African-American. "It does," Woods said. "Growing up, I came up with a name: Cablinasian," referring to the mix of races in his lineage. "I'm just who I am. Whoever you see in front of you," he continued.

"When Tiger admits having a problem with being referred to as an African-American, it is as if he thumbed his nose at an entire race of people," wrote Mary Mitchell of the *Chicago Sun-Times*. "His actions are as conflicting as they are confusing. On the one hand, Tiger Woods gladly accepted the mantle of hero. On the other, he wants to transcend race, at least the African-American part of it. Such a feat would be possible in a color-blind world. In such a place, I would not be a black columnist. There also would be no black politicians, ministers, leaders, athletes or businessmen. There would be no barriers and no barriers to break."

Soon *Time* magazine ran a five-page spread called "I'm Just Who I Am," and other outlets focused primarily on Woods' rejection of being Black. It was a misstep that followed Woods throughout his career, even if he wasn't trying to alienate the Black community, and it set an early stage for how Woods would be covered. Maybe in part because of his father's proclamations, maybe in part because of his own messaging, but Woods was held to a different standard.

This was what made the framing of Woods so difficult. Nobody could live as both an angelic, perfectly behaved agent of change and a twenty-one-year-old kid. Human beings contain some shreds of extremes within them, but Woods didn't have the luxury to be nuanced. Not when he was the face of billion-dollar industries endorsing him. And it meant that whenever he did something to contradict the other side of his identity, he was labeled a hypocrite or a failure to his responsibilities.

When he graced the cover of *GQ* in 1997, he reminded the world he was just an immature kid, as the great writer

Charles P. Pierce wasn't afraid to publish the distasteful jokes Woods made about the size of Black men's genitalia or lesbians in certain sex positions or the Little Rascals asking for fellatio. It became such an issue that IMG had to release a statement from Woods condemning the piece.

From then on out, the public robot version of Woods was born. He'd never trust the media again.

And it would be naive to pretend that the fact that he was Black didn't affect how quickly some were to tear him down. When he returned to the 2010 Masters after his cheating scandal, Augusta National chairman Billy Payne viciously criticized Woods. "It is simply not the degree of his conduct that is so egregious here," Payne said. "It is the fact that he disappointed all of us, and more importantly, our kids and our grandkids. Our hero did not live up to the expectations of the role model we saw for our children." This was the club that didn't have a Black member until 1990, and when the Black star of the sport made mistakes, he was chastised like no other golfer would ever be. *Los Angeles Times* writer Thomas Bonk called it "a public whipping."

This was the challenge. Woods was the biggest star in sports by 2000 now that Jordan had retired. So much of that fame came from the image they created. He played a part in putting himself on the pedestal, so it appeared to be fair game when he fell from it.

And even when he was making mistakes or being criticized, he was still the most popular, and much of that remained with white audiences. In a large feature written in the *Guardian* two weeks before the 2000 Open Championship in Scotland, the writer said, "His appeal is wide, limitless, because he does not threaten anybody. Much has been made in the U.S. of Tiger's achievement in drawing 'minorities' into the game of golf. Yes, certainly. Among the vast hordes that flock, crane, to see him in this least spectator-friendly of sports one does see a small sprinkling of black faces. But that is all. His fans are overwhelmingly white-faced, white bread, middle Americans. Among the many reasons why they like him is the fact that, like Jordan, Woods is not obsessive— as many black Americans are—about his accident of race. No bleeding-heart liberal, no Muhammad Ali, Tiger is no militant for social change."

Like the piece states, Woods did seem to follow the lead of Jordan, the other Nike marketing phenomenon who owned the sports zeitgeist. At the height of his popularity, Jordan was asked to support a Democratic nominee to unseat conservative Senator Jesse Helms, who opposed federal integration policies. Jordan famously responded, "Republicans buy sneakers, too." He was the biggest star in all of sports by a wide margin, and that meant crossover popularity with all races. Jordan capitalized on that to become a billionaire and an NBA team owner. It also meant staying quiet on racial issues.

"I do commend Muhammad Ali for standing up for what he believed in," Jordan said, "but I never thought of myself as an activist. I thought of myself as a basketball player."

Former US President Barack Obama said of the Jordan "sneakers" incident: "I'll be honest, when it was reported that Michael said, 'Republicans buy sneakers, too'—for somebody who was at that time preparing for a career in civil rights law and knowing what Jesse Helms stood for, you would've wanted to see Michael push harder on that. On the other hand, he was still trying to figure out, 'How am I managing this image that has been created around me, and how do I live up to it?'"

Woods was figuring out how to handle race, too. He was learning how to wield the power of his enormous fame, especially when race was not a driving issue for him yet he represented it to so many others. His hope was, like Mitchell said, to transcend race.

Yet two weeks later in those same *Guardian* pages, the day before the beginning of the Open, an English financial adviser was quoted saying, "I am not backing Tiger Woods. He is an arrogant, ethnic fellow." His buddy seated next to him shot him a nervous glare.

In 2000, Tiger Woods was the most talked about, discussed, and debated man in all of sports. So, in the span of any week, he could both be condemned for his race and beloved because he supposedly didn't care about it.

"Woods has been a reluctant hero for Black America," said Andscape writer Farrell Evans, who covered Woods' career for *Sports Illustrated* and ESPN.com, "while looming as a god over the sport. His rejection of Louis' social and political mantle for Black athletes has been painful for many in Black America, who saw him as a source of racial pride and a champion over decades of racism in the game of golf."

Chapter Six

———

THE OLD COURSE

It was once a place of refuge, bands of sheep huddled together in the sandy soil to hide from the mighty North Sea winds. The malleable pieces of earth at St Andrews depressed beneath them hundreds of years ago, enough so that the shepherds who first played golf along the Scottish coast would find the hole more difficult to play when a ball landed in those sandy depressions. Soon the bug became a feature. Golf courses purposely designed lands to mimic the holes those sheep left. And when you stand inside one of them now, you do not go in it for refuge. You plead to get out in one piece.

There are 112 of them now. Some are as deep as ten feet. Some have lips that rise fifteen feet. The sodded walls are rowed into lines that make them feel like prison bars. The grass above and around them is sloped so that any ball nearby will roll into them. The bunkers at the Old Course at St Andrews are golf's great villain at the ancestral home of the sport. The game was first played on these sandy stretches linking the land to the ocean in 1552. It is where Old Tom Morris was born in 1821, where he learned the game and became head greenskeeper and club professional. It's where his son, Tom Morris Jr., was born and where he died, too, the eight Open Championships between them. And in the five hundred years since those links were formed, golfers have made pilgrimages to play this piece of history in the oldest college town in Scotland.

And it's those bunkers that can ruin a day or a life. They are the bunkers that Bobby Jones took four swings from, failing to ever get his ball out of the sand before picking up his ball and moving on. He finished his round but didn't turn his card in because of the incident on the 11th hole, disqualifying Jones from the 1921 Open Championship.

It's those bunkers that Nicklaus found in 1995, landing in the 14th hole's famous "Hell Bunker." He took four shots to get out of it before accepting a ten for a quadruple bogey. Most recommend to simply take the loss and hit it backward to escape.

And it's those bunkers that left O'Meara stuck for eight straight failed shots during a 2000 practice round before throwing it out with his hands. These bunkers have always been one of the Old Course's great signature features, with on average six per hole of different types like pot bunkers, revetted bunkers, and hidden bunkers, but before this 2000 Open the grounds crew upped their game and made them seemingly impossible.

"They outdid themselves on the bunkers," Nicklaus said before the Open. "They're very, very, very difficult. Toughest I've ever seen."

Even Woods worried about them. He practiced from them all week, even spending time lining shots with a 5-iron into the front wall to see if he could ricochet a ball off it to safety, nearly hitting himself in the face a few times.

Those damned bunkers were the story of the week leading into that millennial Open Championship. An attendant with a massive seven-foot rake followed each group, an ominous foreshadowing in the backs of their minds. At one point that week, Mark Calcavecchia and Sergio García had to bring out the putter and slap the ball away from the wall just to be able to hit. Players were terrified.

Eighteen holes. One hundred twelve bunkers per round. Four hundred forty-eight bunkers total across seventy-two holes. And somehow, Tiger didn't find one the entire tournament.

———

Steve Williams took extra pride in caddying St Andrews. He often called it a "caddie's course." Links courses are these seemingly unscientific, unpredictable pieces of land in which golfers can't just play straight and simple like on so many flat American courses. They require knowledge. They require creativity. They require lessons learned from painful mistakes on previous trips. Up until 1995, they didn't even have sprinklers in the fairway at St Andrews, and there wasn't a tree in sight. So, caddies like Williams had to use random landmarks to figure out distances. Maybe a land post on one hole. The corner of a building on another. Maybe he'd use a mound or a bunker. On the famous stretch of land that serves as both the 1st and 18th fairways, he learned he could line up the ninth lamppost with the corner of a certain building to help measure.

And in his major victories with Woods, he took even more pride in that work. He'd get to the Old Course at 4 a.m. sunup to begin scouting each day and often see other caddies finishing up all-night drinking sessions at the Jigger Inn. In that dawn work, he'd often figure out game plans for how Woods could attack certain holes or avoid certain bunkers.

It was with that combination of a well-prepared caddie and golfer at his peak that they attacked this Old Course by not quite attacking. Tiger played patient, intelligent golf. He didn't make any mistakes. Woods opened with eight consecutive pars before finally birdieing 9 and 10, finishing with a bogey-free 67 to put himself at the top of the leaderboard. In the afternoon, his contemporary Ernie Els shot a 66 to snag the solo lead.

But most mere mortals have variance across four rounds. What made Woods so infuriating was the way he didn't. Els had a cold putting day on Friday and shot just a 72 while others like Sergio García and David Toms played their way ahead. But like so many majors before and after, Woods created his gap with the field by that second round. As he teed off, Nicklaus walked down the stairs by the clubhouse right past him as he completed his final Open Championship round while missing the cut. His heir apparent then began, shooting a 66 to reach 11-under par, three ahead of Toms in solo second.

Tiger didn't score an eagle in all that time. He just played the course down the middle, never finding a bunker and never putting himself in too much trouble. He hit creative 100-yard putts from the fairway for tap-ins. He pitched out of the rough on the iconic 17th "Road Hole" and put it past the hole, rolling up the hill and coming back down for an impressive save. His opponents would almost rather him annihilate the course. It was more deflating watching the course fail to annihilate him.

Three-time major winner Nick Price could hardly light his cigarette in the moments after playing the second round with Woods. *Sports Illustrated*'s Steve Rushin wrote of Price recollecting witnessing this performance, speaking in fragments as he kept trying to light the cigarette.

"He's on cruise, man," said Price, desperately flicking a disposable lighter in the manner of someone who had just witnessed a riveting calamity. "I'm telling you, he hasn't even tried any shots yet . . . (flick!) . . . I've seen him mishit only three shots this week . . . (flick!) . . . I played like that once in my life, at the PGA . . . (flick!) . . . He's played like that four or five times now and will do it 20 more times." Price finally produced a flame and sparked a cigarette. "Tiger cut a three-wood off the tee at 17 today, and I smoked a driver," he said, exhaling. "He was a yard past me."

Scotland became obsessed with Woods, the man achieving things they thought only Old Tom Morris could do against fields of farmers. A record 230,000 people attended the tournament, and the overwhelming majority of those were following Woods to get a look at this foreign object.

———

Tiger has heard people telling him what the best shot of his career was for years. Some he disagrees with. Some he thinks are in the conversation. And in 2000, he played some of the best golf ever played, so plenty of shots make the all-time list. But Woods only remembered hitting one shot that year that he'd call perfect. And it came from the 14th fairway at the Old Course.

That 14th hole is one of the trickiest at St Andrews. The "Hell Bunker" sits in front of the green. There's out of bounds to the right. And the shot into the green is blind, so to aim for it you have to pick a line to aim at and hope you're right. Much of the beauty of St Andrews comes from the Gothic churches and cathedrals and the beautiful churches in the distance. Well, in Williams' scouting walks, he spent a great deal of time determining the best lines for when Woods would need this shot from the 14th fairway.

Williams kept pointing at this one spire of a cathedral, but Woods couldn't quite tell which he was talking about. They had to go back and forth to make sure they had the same object in mind before finally hitting the shot. "It took some explanation," Williams joked.

They finally settled on the correct spire, and Woods stopped to visualize the ball's flight and how it should respond upon landing—like he does before every shot. From a tight lie, Woods then launched a little right-to-left draw shot into the left-to-right wind and carried it 260 yards and safely onto the right side of the green.

From the moment he made contact, Woods twirled his club and dryly said, "Is that the one you're talking about?" while staring straight and walking toward the green for the two-putt for birdie. "The ball never left that line and the shot turned out exactly as I had planned," Woods said of his rare perfect shot.

That sixth birdie of the day gave him a six-shot lead. It wasn't like Pebble Beach where the rest of the field cratered from the daunting conditions. No, players like Thomas Bjorn and David Duval played excellent Saturday golf to reach 10-under par. Northern Irishman Darren Clarke lurked at 9-under. This time, though, it was Woods' failure to make a mistake that pushed him ahead. He was just so steady. Even the rare bogey, like he did on 17 at the Road Hole that round, was followed by a birdie on 18 to end the round 16-under through 54 holes.

"That week he played up there with the best I've seen him play," Williams said.

———

John Wells was the man tasked with following Woods all of the final round with the large rake in case a ball went into the bunker. And through three rounds, he still hadn't had to use it. "I hope I get to use my rake," Wells told a cameraman, "because my money was on Darren Clarke on Thursday, and if I get to use my rake a bit that might come in."

Woods wore his signature Sunday red shirt to signify it was time to close out a tournament, paired with his good friend and apparent rival Duval, who still sought his first major. Duval had briefly taken world No. 1 from Woods and finished top ten in seven of his last ten majors, and early in that final round he birdied two holes to get within four of Woods. If anyone could catch him in 2000, the assumption was that Duval was the guy.

Duval then missed a remarkably short birdie putt on the 5th hole, and historically that meant things were over in a duel with Woods. You cannot miss your chances against Tiger. Duval knew that as well as anyone. But he wouldn't go away. He still cut the lead to three, and it remained that way as they made the turn to 10.

But Wells kept holding that rake, and he kept logging zeros on his yellow sheet under Woods because he never had to record a usage. He wouldn't make a mistake, and on the back nine Duval finally faltered. He missed a chance to cut the lead with a birdie on 10, and his collapse soon began. He found multiple bunkers and put himself so near the bunker wall on 17 that he had to just knock it backward to even have a chance at pitching out. His back nine 43 dropped him all the way to 11th place. And as he and Woods embraced on the 18th tee, Woods whispered in Duval's ear, "You're a true champion, and walk off like a champion." Duval won the Open the next year for his lone major victory.

But first, Woods had to walk that 18th fairway and step over the Swilken Bridge while the massive crowds broke contain over Her Majesty's Marshals and flooded the fairway behind him. It was a scene reminiscent of Phil Mickelson's 2021 win at Kiawah, the crowd practically carrying Woods to the green.

Woods, twenty-four, won his career Grand Slam. Finally, because in the moments after his win, he said, "I thought I'd be at this point faster than it took." Pay no mind to the fact that he did it two years faster than anyone had ever done it, including Nicklaus. Woods finished 19-under par, eight shots ahead of the second-place Bjorn.

Twelve months earlier, Woods was stuck at one career major and under constant criticism. Since then, he'd won three of the last four majors played. He'd won the last two by a combined twenty-three shots. All-time great Tom Watson said during the run, "He has raised the bar to a level only he can jump. He's something supernatural."

Earl still wasn't there, just like he wasn't at Pebble Beach. His health was declining, and he and Woods agreed Tiger needed to be his own man. One person who was standing there was Kultida. She was the one who walked every hole of every course with Woods throughout his youth and so much of his professional career. She was the one who ingrained a killer instinct in him and removed so much of the sentimentality Earl overflowed with. So it's no surprise that she didn't get emotional when he won most tournaments.

"Even when Tiger won at the Masters first time, and the old man was sobbing, I was very happy but did not break down," she said. "At US Open at Pebble Beach, on Sunday when all the people on the fairway bowed to him, I think, 'That's nice.' But that's all."

But for some reason, it was this moment at the Old Course that broke her down. She cried as she watched him make his way to the green, as her son reached the career Grand Slam overseas.

"When he was coming up the last hole of the Old Course, which is so much history, and all the people are waving and applauding, and I thought, 'That is my son.'"

Woods was then given the Claret Jug, holding it in both hands on the green with his head tilted around staring at it. Unlike at Pebble, where his smile gave off a sense of routine happiness like he knew he'd win, he couldn't stop staring at the jug with a solemn face. He mouthed "Wow" to himself while the cameras flashed. He'd really done it. He'd won them all.

———

Chapter Seven

TIGER WOODS IS PLAYING A DIFFERENT SPORT

In the aftermath of the annihilation, as a twenty-four-year-old star only four years into his career just lapped the field at consecutive majors by twenty-three combined shots, it was left to Nicklaus to try to make sense of it all.

"He has to have challengers for the whole thing to be right," Nicklaus warned a room of reporters at St Andrews. "It's a bad story if there aren't any challengers. You guys won't have anything to write about."

The best player in the world changed his entire swing, took a slight dip for two years, and then came back so dominant that there was no evidence any golfer could beat him if Woods was on his game. And he was just beginning.

When Woods ran away with his record-breaking win at Pebble Beach, it was simply the best tournament ever played. But it was one tournament. When he did it again at the next major, the entire sport seemed to have a collective thought piercing through their heads: *We're all fucked.*

"He's the best who ever played," Mark Calcavecchia said that Sunday, "and he's twenty-four."

"He is the best player in the world by a long, long way and we have got to raise our standards to join his," Colin Montgomerie said. "We have got to go up to his and we are all trying. We are all failing, but we are all trying."

"He's got to leave a few for his friends, doesn't he?" Jean Van de Velde said. "He can't have them all."

"If you put Old Tom Morris with Tiger Woods," Els said, "[Woods] would probably beat him by 80 shots right now. The guy is unbelievable, man. I'm running out of words. Give me a break."

He'd suddenly won fourteen tournaments in just over a year. Within Nicklaus' thoughts on the state of golf were more references to all the greats Nicklaus had to beat in his era, while Woods wasn't facing those types of accomplished winners. To Nicklaus' credit, he said multiple times that those types of rivals would come and eventually Woods' wins would gain more prestige, but it felt like another dig at Woods' competition. He was implying the wins carried less weight.

This is the challenge golf historians have and will continue to struggle with going forward when trying to contextualize Woods and his era. Were his competitors that much weaker? Or was Woods so good he rendered an entire generation of great golfers obsolete?

Because there's no denying the types of players Nicklaus beat—and who beat him. His rise came in tandem with Arnold Palmer. Meanwhile Nicklaus, Gary Player, and Lee Trevino went at it over and over. When Nicklaus continued to win and compete into his late thirties and forties, he had multiple epic duels with Tom Watson.

While in Woods' general run of major domination from 1997 to 2008, nobody ever came face-to-face with the big cat and outplayed him. Until 2009, nobody ever caught Woods when he had at least a share of the 54-hole lead at a major. And the man who ended the streak was an obscure Cinderella story by the name of Y. E. Yang. For roughly a decade, either Woods had it or he didn't. It was that simple.

It's why the story of Miguel Ángel Jiménez at Pebble asking, "Can you tell me when the playoff starts for the other tournament between me and Ernie?" is so important and, in a way, heartbreaking. An entire generation of great players didn't seem to have a chance. Woods entered majors with odds as low as 2-to-1 where it was a sincere conversation whether bettors should take Tiger or the field in a given tournament. And considering the differences in those eras, one can't help but wonder if those greats were just as good as Nicklaus' contemporaries because of the way Woods won. Keep in mind, Nicklaus was also a 2-to-1 favorite at the 1972 Open.

Even during the Tiger Slam run, it frustrated golfers the way Woods' greatness was discussed in a way that insulted the rest around him.

"Certainly any time you write a golf story right now, seems like, you know, Tiger is going to be in there somewhere if he is competing and I understand that," Duval said in 2000. "But Tiger Woods' exceptional year doesn't make Davis Love any worse of a player or anybody else any worse of a player. That is the only thing that I have seen that I think has happened in the last twelve months that has been a little unfair."

Ernie Els. Phil Mickelson. Vijay Singh. David Duval. Colin Montgomerie. Davis Love III. Sergio García. So many more. How different would we view their legacies if Woods didn't exist or played in a different time?

"He demolished poor Ernie," Butch Harmon said. "He demolished Davis Love. He demolished Mickelson. All these guys that were playing so good, he just demolished them. He made them feel inferior."

Mickelson has won six major championships in his career, and that run came after he turned thirty-three and after a decade of being known as the best golfer without a major. Mickelson not winning from 1993 to 2003 wasn't exactly all because of Woods, as Woods didn't truly become the force he was until 1999. Like many before him, Mickelson just took time to put it all together and learn how to finish. When he did, he won five majors over the next nine years, and in 2021 he added to his legacy by winning the PGA Championship at fifty years, eleven months, and seven days, the oldest major winner in history.

Mickelson, the controversial yet beloved Lefty, is

the only golfer other than Woods to reach six majors since Nick Faldo did it in 1996. And Faldo was the first since Trevino in 1984. So, yes, that era had more elite major winners: Nicklaus 18, Player 9, Watson 8, Palmer 7, Trevino 6. But it was also just that, a different era. There is far more competition and balance in the twenty-first century—other than Woods playing on a different level—which is why professional golf currently has some of the most talented golfers in history, like Brooks Koepka, Rory McIlroy, Jordan Spieth, Scottie Scheffler, Dustin Johnson, Jon Rahm, Justin Thomas, Bryson DeChambeau, Xander Schauffele, and Collin Morikawa, all with two to five majors but none with more. Nobody other than Woods has reached seven since Watson in 1983.

Years later, Mickelson would say of the comparison people tried to make in their rivalry: "The reality is, even if I play at the top of my game for the rest of my career and achieve my goals—let's say, win 50 tournaments and 10 majors, pretty difficult to do, since I'd need 20 more wins, including seven more majors—I still won't get to where Tiger is right now. So I won't compare myself with him. It makes no sense. I'm playing perhaps the greatest player ever while he's in his prime. It sucks losing to him, for sure, but it's a great challenge. I love trying to beat him."

Mickelson won five majors while Woods was still fully active. Only one of those had Woods within two shots, and that was the 2005 PGA Championship, where Woods shot a 68 to jump up the leaderboard on the final day to get within two. He never truly beat him in a major when they were in a head-to-head duel.

It was Mickelson, though, who ended Woods' historic six tournament streak from 1999 to 2000. Playing in the Buick Invitational at Torrey Pines, Woods came from seven shots back to tie Mickelson on the final day, only to bogey the next two holes and fade away.

"I didn't back off. I didn't dog it out there," Woods said that day. "I just hung in there. For some reason I didn't hit the ball as crisp today as I needed to."

"I wasn't out to end the streak. I don't want to be the bad guy," Mickelson said. "I just wanted to win the tournament."

Over the course of his career, seventy-seven different golfers (many who did it multiple times) finished second to Woods in a PGA Tour event. Twenty-nine of those were major winners. But no golfer finished second to Woods more often than Els, the Big Easy, who was runner-up to Woods a record five times.

Mickelson may go down as Woods' greatest rival, but Els will always be the one who Woods took the most from. The South African won four majors across three decades, won more than seventy tournaments across the world, and reached world No. 1 three different times. He is one of the greatest golfers of all time.

But in 2000 alone, Els finished second to Woods four times, and each was a big-time tournament like the US Open, the Open Championship, the Memorial, and the Mercedes Championship in Hawaii. And in all of Els' four major wins, only one of them came with Woods in the mix, and even that was a three-shot difference in the 2012 Open Championship.

"I had quite a few run-ins with him in majors," Els recalled. "It wasn't really very close, but I finished second to him many times. Personally, I could have obviously won a couple more. He was so special, he's so special, and he absolutely changed the game. He got us to really elevate our games, brought so much more attention to the sport, and obviously a lot more dollars to play for. So we've got to thank him. But, you know, I could have had a couple more, definitely, without him around."

But there's another element involved in all of this that is more difficult to pin down. It's not as simple as who is better than whom at golf. It's what has become known as the "Tiger Effect."

Tiger had a different level of intensity on the golf course, the product of a child raised with his father's military psychology techniques, his mother's killer instinct, and working with psychologists and hypnotists to create the perfect zone on a course. That demeanor could affect opponents in its own right, but the Tiger Effect was rooted in the compounding nature of seeing Woods rip their hearts out too many times. Eventually, when Woods was even remotely in reach, players cratered.

He wore a red polo on every Sunday no matter what. That Sunday red became his signature, signifying a hunter out for blood. Each epic photo of Woods winning a title includes him wearing that red, and it carried its own weight. Opponents feared Woods when he wore red.

"He had the intimidation of when people saw him and he wasn't at the top of the leaderboard and all of a sudden he's making birdies and they're all looking up going, 'Oh, shit. Here he comes,'" Harmon said. "They'd go down and he'd keep going up."

This seemingly anecdotal phenomenon interested Northwestern researcher Jennifer Brown to the point that she conducted an analytical study of how Woods' contemporaries played with Woods in the field called "Quitters Never Win: The (Adverse) Incentive Effects of Competing with Superstars." She adjusted for factors such as weather, purse size, and the prestige level of events and only counted players who made the cut.

She found players performed an average of 0.8 strokes worse when Woods was in the field. In majors, the top twenty players on tour played 0.6 strokes worse in the first round alone. Brown even dug deeper to see if this was because players were more aggressive in trying to match Woods, and she found zero statistical evidence that players were more aggressive. She also found that the disparity wasn't simply because of the pressure of big events, as they played worse in big tournaments when Woods was there compared to other equal tournaments that Woods missed.

In 102 of 134 events in a seven-year span, Brown argues Woods would have either dropped to a tied position or below other players than he did if these players performed to their usual capabilities without Woods. Her study found the Tiger Effect led to him winning just under $1 million extra earnings per year.

Former world No. 1 Adam Scott said in 2020: "If anyone was playing at that time and they were being honest there's no doubt he made a big difference . . . I think I would have told myself to come up with a strategy to block out exactly what Tiger was doing and making us all kind of feel slightly inferior to him."

Chris Perry said in 2000, "You really have to watch when you play with him that you don't get wrapped up in what he is doing because you have our own stuff to do but it is mind-boggling what this guy can do with a golf ball."

McIlroy, one of the many current golfers who grew up idolizing Woods, said, "Just sorta having that little glimpse of red in your eye. A hundred percent. I mean, he knows that he intimidates people and it's like, 'I'm going to make you feel my presence.'"

Harmon remembers other pros coming up to him on the range and asking if they could film him hitting some shots. Other professionals were openly trying to study him! Harmon would look at Woods as if to say, "I'm not answering that." Woods would calmly say, "No, that's OK. Get a few films," and get back to work like it didn't matter to him.

"The problem was unless you were climbing into his body you couldn't do what he was doing," Harmon said with a chuckle.

ESPN anchor and former Golf Channel reporter Scott Van Pelt is adamant that Woods' shocking 2019 Masters win after years of surgeries, scandal, and aging could be traced back to the Tiger Effect. The tournament was arguably decided by Francesco Molinari, Tony Finau, and Koepka all hitting into the water on the famously tricky 12th hole, a short par 3 over water with wind swirling in the corner of the property. Woods was the one to play conservative and safely land it on the green.

But the two golfers most associated with Woods robbing their primes are the two golfers who deny any feeling of an effect. Els and Mickelson both think Woods made them better, not the other way around.

"Had Tiger not come around, I don't feel I would have pushed myself to achieve what I ended up achieving, because he forced everybody to get the best out of themselves," Mickelson said. "He forced everybody to work a little bit harder. He forced everybody to look at fitness as a big part of the game of golf, and I think that's actually helped me with longevity . . . to elongate the career. And I feel like that's been a big part of it and he was a big influence on that."

Els agreed, but he did admit one thing.

"People ask me this question a lot: 'What separated Tiger from us?'

"There's a lot of things, but the one real factor was his intensity on the first tee. On the first tee you just want to get in the round and see how things are, testing out the waters of the competition. Hopefully by 4 or 5 you are even par or one under and get into the tournament. A lot of us were like that, but Tiger, he was different. On the first tee he was ready to go. He was ready to absolutely strangle the golf course and get to the field eventually and really take down the tournament. He wasn't there to mess around. He didn't play too many events but when he played he was ready to go."

But for all the pontificating on mental effects and the quality of his competition, it risks downplaying the actual golf Woods played. This isn't a team sport where a team can score at will on a weaker defense. It is about one person trying to finish in as few shots as possible.

The website DataGolf.com, an industry leader in quantifying golf performance, had an offseason project to better judge the greatest seasons in golf history. It attempted to combine shot by shot performance via strokes gained with the relative difficulty of each given tournament in a season to better understand who truly rose to the highest level. It created a metric called DG Points and traced results back to the 1980s.

For reference, the best ever non-Tiger season was Scottie Scheffler's 2024, in which he won nine tournaments worldwide and dominated competitors in overall strokes gained. He earned 173.5 DG Points. Vijay Singh's nine-win 2004 earned 160.5. Jordan Spieth's two-major winning 2015 earned 158.

In 2000, Woods earned 217.5 DG Points.

Here are some other examples, though, of just how good Woods was on the course.

- In 2000, Woods scored just one round higher than 73 for an entire season. That's 80 rounds of tournament golf. His only round where he scored higher? A 75 on a day where the course average was 75.59.
- The gap between the 2nd best player and the 25th best player in greens in regulation was about 3 percent in 2000. All the best players in the world lived in that 69 to 72 percent range with their approach play. The tour average was 65 percent. Woods found his greens in regulation 75 percent of the time, the same gap between No. 2 and No. 25 golfers in the category. That meant he hardly had to scramble that year compared to his foes, and even in that category his short game was so good that he was third on tour, saving par or better 67 percent of the time when he missed a green.
- Putting average is far from a perfect stat, but most advanced metrics didn't arrive until the mid-2000s.

It measures how many putts you need from greens in regulation. Woods finished second on tour behind only Brad Faxon, a man who now teaches putting to the best players in the world.

- Total driving combines a player's ability to both drive with distance and accuracy off the tee. For example, John Daly was the only player who hit it farther than Woods, but Daly ranked 191st in total driving because he was so erratic off the tee like most long drivers at the time. Woods ranked first in total driving, the only golfer in the world who ranked top 5 in distance *and* top 25 in total driving.

- The top 10 players in birdie average per round all averaged between 4 and 4.26 birdies per 18 holes. Woods averaged 4.92.

- The adjusted scoring average metric determines the average score of the field in each round played and adjusts the players' scoring average accordingly. In 2000, the second best adjusted average was from Phil Mickelson with 69.254. Every golfer ranked from 2nd to 100th averaged between his 69.254 and 71.254. Woods averaged 67.

- One last one to drive it home: Take the 2021 strokes gained leaders in the four main golfing categories—

off-the-tee, approach, around the green, and putting. In 2021, Bryson DeChambeau gained 1.162 strokes per round off the tee. Collin Morikawa gained 1.17 in approach. Kevin Na gained 0.702 around the green. And Louis Oosthuizen gained 0.764 on the greens. If you combine them all to create essentially the hypothetical perfect all-around golfer in 2021, they'd gain 3.8 strokes on the field. In 2000, Woods gained 3.83 strokes per round.

———

Bobby Jones didn't come around much in those days. He was sixty-three and weakening, spinal troubles ailing him such that he could hardly host. By the 1965 Masters, Jones let his old friend and colleague Clifford Roberts take on most of his duties. But it was a beautiful spring day, and Jones felt well enough to make a rare appearance on the course and camp out by the 15th green. One after another, golfers who likely didn't get to see Jones play walked over to pay their respects before walking to the 16th tee. And from that spot, Jones watched as Nicklaus holed out for birdie on 15.

Tiger Woods' epic run of four major championships began at beautiful Pebble Beach, one of golf's most iconic venues along the Pacific Ocean and Carmel Bay. Woods, playing the new Nike Tour Accuracy golf ball, won the 2000 US Open by a record-breaking fifteen-shot margin. *Jonathan Ferrey*

Claude "Butch" Harmon Jr. is, other than Tiger's mother, Kultida, the primary constant figure throughout the Tiger Slam run. Harmon started coaching Woods when Woods was an amateur in 1993, and stayed by his side until they parted ways in 2004. While Earl Woods was known to be heavily involved in Tiger's game, he famously said to Harmon in 1993, "I'll make a deal with you. You don't try to be his father and I won't try to be his coach." *Harry How*

At the home of golf with some of the most famous and difficult bunkers in the world, Tiger Woods did not find a single bunker in seventy-two holes at St Andrews while running away with an eight-stroke Open Championship victory. *Harry How*

Above left: In a playoff at the 2000 PGA Championship at Valhalla Golf Club in Louisville, Kentucky, Woods sunk an essential birdie putt and felt such confidence that he strutted and pointed at the ball well before it went in the hole. It is one of the more famous images in Woods' iconography, and the putt that ultimately won him his third major in a row. *David Cannon*

Above right: Caddie Steve Williams was new to Tiger Woods' bag in 1999, and it was when they won their first major championship together at the 1999 PGA Championship that Woods truly learned to trust Williams. Needing par on the seventeenth hole, Woods asked Williams for help with a read and Williams said, "Inside left." Woods said, "Perfect," and made the putt to beat Sergio García. *Craig Jones*

Opposite top: Jack Nicklaus, the man whose eighteen majors were the lifelong pursuit of Woods, was often the person downplaying Woods' blowout victories because of what he considered weaker competition. After playing thirty-six holes with Woods at the 2000 PGA Championship, Nicklaus repeated the famous line Bobby Jones said of him: "He's playing a game I'm not familiar with." *Jeff Haynes*

One of the more well-known sporting fathers of all time, Earl Woods began working with Tiger Woods at golf before he was a year old. He was a constant and often controversial figure during his rise and before health issues led to him appearing less by 2000. Earl died on May 3, 2006. *Robert Sullivan*

As Tiger Woods made his final putt to win the 2001 Masters and waited for Phil Mickelson to finish his round, he hid his face as he broke into tears. The enormity of winning four majors in a row finally hit him. "I just started thinking, you know, I don't have any more shots to play," Woods said. "I'm done." *Timothy Clary*

While Earl Woods got the most attention throughout Tiger Woods' career, most people close to Tiger say it was his mother, Kultida, who instilled the killer instinct and competitor into the fifteen-time major champion. Kultida followed nearly every round and tournament of his career, even appearing at TGL events in winter 2025, before her death on February 4, 2025. *Mike Fiala*

Tiger Woods kisses the Claret Jug after winning the 2000 Open Championship, becoming the youngest golfer to complete the career Grand Slam with all four major championships. At twenty-four, he did it even sooner than Jack Nicklaus. *Popperfoto*

Jones was there to see Nicklaus playing Augusta better than any man ever had, breaking the tournament record by three shots at 17-under par. Nicklaus played the kind of invincible golf that left other greats shrugging their shoulders. Palmer and Player, tied for second place, scored so well they would have won twenty-three of the previous twenty-eight Masters.

So as Jones held court at the presentation ceremony and spoke, he said, "I have an aversion to superlatives, but this was the greatest performance in all golfing history."

The crowd then died down and Jones kept speaking to a smaller group after the ceremony when he added another thought now etched in golf lore.

"Palmer and Player played superbly," he said. "Nicklaus plays a game with which I am not familiar."

Fast forward thirty-five years, and Nicklaus was just three years younger than Jones was then. He was in far better shape (he's still alive at the time of this book's publication), but he was ready to end his playing career. And throughout the 2000 season, the story of Nicklaus' conclusion was told in tandem with Woods' rise. He finished his 36th holes to miss the cut seemingly right as Woods teed off at both the US and British Opens. Both times it felt like a passing of the torch moment, and both times Woods went on to convincingly win.

Woods grew up with all of Nicklaus' achievements posted to his wall. He watched Nicklaus' famous and final major victory at the 1986 Masters as a boy and knew that was the milestone he hoped to chase. They first connected when Woods was a teenager and went on to share a bond as the lone golfers who could truly understand each other.

But the two had never played a tournament round together. That was until the 2000 PGA Championship, Nicklaus' final PGA appearance, at Valhalla Golf Club in Louisville, a course Nicklaus designed. Nicklaus was grouped with the last two major champs, Vijay Singh and Woods.

"It's time to pass the baton," Nicklaus said of their pairing. "This guy's really good."

Woods looked looser those two days. He looked free. Maybe it was from the high of two monumental wins. Maybe it was because, for two days, he wasn't the only attraction every fan homed in on. Many of the fans were there to see Nicklaus one last time and cheer for him. They joked around together, Woods seeming so different from the laser-focused machine he often displays at majors.

Woods jumped out for a share of the first round lead

with Scott Dunlap after a 66, and on Friday he took the solo lead at 11-under par. But on the 36th hole together, Nicklaus needed an eagle to make the cut.

They shared a sentimental moment as Nicklaus wrapped up his round, but Woods cut him off to tell him Nicklaus needed to finish strong. He had looked up to Nicklaus his entire life because he was a competitor, the kind of competitor who didn't want anybody to catch his records. He was finally playing a tournament round with the Golden Bear. He wanted to see him go for it.

Nicklaus hit a perfect pitch just left of the pin and spun it back right along the edge of the cup, landing inches from the hole. It was a vintage Nicklaus shot, but it was time to call it a week and a career. He putted in for birdie and missed the cut. His time on the course was finished, but Woods was just beginning.

"He's playing a game I'm not familiar with," Nicklaus said, repeating Jones' famous line. Nicklaus added, "And I'm playing a game I'm not familiar with either."

Woods was playing a game of golf that the best players in the world couldn't match. Yet right as the golf world panicked that he was something greater than human, an unsuspecting golfer from Woods' past was waiting for him.

His name was Bob May.

Chapter Eight

THE UNSUSPECTING RIVAL

Tiger Woods and Bob May had been circling around each other for longer than either knew, two Southern California prodigies living parallel lives on the path to one epic weekend in Louisville. They were born seven years apart less than twenty miles from each other. They both dominated the California record books and racked up junior titles. They both were the top college recruits in the country on the path to big things. But when they collided in August 2000, they met as two golfers so foreign to each other, a reminder of the ways a journey can take detours and side streets on the road to one monumental moment.

On one side was a six-foot-one, 180-pound, twenty-four-year-old sculpture of a perfect golfer shattering records the sport never thought could be touched. On the other was a five-foot-seven, 155-pound, thirty-one-year-old journeyman who had just earned his PGA Tour card back after a few years in Europe. One man was *supposed* to win every major he played, while very few casual fans had even heard of May.

The media understandably labeled this the ultimate David vs. Goliath story, and it would be understandable to think this. May had no PGA Tour wins. It was his first season even playing in most majors. In a year in which Mickelson, Els, Duval, and Love couldn't match Woods in his ascent or even compete in majors, it made no sense that it was May in this position, in the final group with Woods just one shot back with eighteen holes to go in the PGA Championship.

There were just two people who truly understood that this was not quite the David and Goliath story it seemed on the surface. One was May, a man with deep self-confidence and a drive to make good on his full potential. The other was Woods.

Steve Williams knew very little about May, but as the two were paired, it was Woods who whispered in Williams' ear, "This guy won't back down."

———

May wasn't the kid picking up his dad's clubs in the garage at nine months old. No, his parents weren't golfers at all. His career was not designed in a lab or structured from a young age. He didn't go on TV at two or win tournaments at five. It wasn't until he stayed at his aunt's house one night when he was about seven and the next morning his aunt and her husband invited him to go golfing with them. They bought him a little 7-iron, a club that he carried around everywhere and still keeps in his home to this day.

One day, when his parents weren't home, May watched golf on TV and noticed the pros taking these huge divots in the ground. He walked out in front of his home outside Los Angeles with his 7-iron in hand and began hacking into the ground. The dichondra grass substitute was torn to pieces all across the yard, while May had no clue that he was doing something wrong. His neighbor walked by and saw.

"You are so dead," the neighbor said.

"Why?" the naive seven-year-old asked.

When his (understandably upset) father came home, he told May that if he wanted to play this game, he'd need lessons. He drove him to the nearest driving range and found a coach. By nine, May was winning tournaments. By eleven or twelve, he quit baseball and soccer and committed his life to golf. He was obsessed, and in turn he worked at it constantly because he enjoyed it so much.

May was Tiger Woods before Tiger Woods, at least in Southern California. He won at least one AJGA tournament six years in a row, a record that still stands today. He won eight junior tournaments total, the same number as Woods. He was the youngest golfer to ever qualify for the U.S. Amateur. The PGA named him national player of the year twice, and *Sports Illustrated* put him on its "Faces in the Crowd" before eventually naming him player of the year as well.

May was *the guy*. The golf world always has *the guy*. Quite often it has *the woman*, too. It's the next person anticipated to be a star golfer for the foreseeable future. It was Scott Verplank. Then it was May. Then Mickelson. Then Woods. Later there was McIlroy. Then Rickie Fowler. Then Spieth. Then Jon Rahm. Nowadays it's Ludvig Åberg, Nick Dunlap, and Gordon Sargent.

But when you're in it, when you're the guy, you can

never imagine a moment you won't be. Life is all in front of you, and there's no scar tissue creating doubt in your mind. There is not even the slightest reason to think that this success will one day end.

"I thought I'd always be one of golf's great golfers," May said.

He has this memory stuck in his head of hanging out before an AJGA event in Lake Tahoe, a tournament he won three times in his junior career. He was talking with some parents, including his own, when one of the dads asked, "Hey Bobby, what score is gonna win this tournament?"

"What I shoot," May said without missing a beat.

His father shuddered in the corner, likely thinking, Here he goes again. May, of course, won the tournament by double digits.

"When you're playing good, you feel invincible," he admits. When he runs into some of those parents now, he embarrassedly jokes about how cocky he was, to which the parents always say, "You always backed it up at least." Because he worked hard, adamant that nobody would ever enter a tournament more prepared.

The first time it even registered to him that maybe, one day, this could all be taken from him was when he got hurt while water skiing as a teenager. He felt helpless without the game. There weren't computers, so he had to call friends around the country to find out who shot what and how everyone was doing at events. And he'd always ask how Ernie Els did, because Els, a year beneath him, was the top international amateur from South Africa while May was the top dog in the States. Els was his measuring stick. When he returned from the slight muscle injury, he immediately got to work because he was paranoid Els would gain ground in the winter since that was summertime in South Africa.

May chose to play golf at the collegiate powerhouse Oklahoma State, and it was then that his rise slowed down.

"When I went to school, I was probably the best player in the country," May said, "and when I left school I was not. It really took so much of my time to try to stay eligible."

He didn't learn it until the final semester of his senior year, but May suffers from dyslexia. He never felt like a dumb person, he said. He could keep up a conversation with anyone and had good common sense, but he struggled with tests and reading. When it got so bad he risked losing eligibility, it only made him stress and tighten up more.

That struggle took so much of his focus that he leveled out while peers surpassed him. He was still a top college player, earning an invitation to the 1991 US Walker Cup team, an event that serves as essentially the collegiate Ryder Cup but against Great Britain and Ireland. He was on a star-studded team with names like Mickelson and Duval, and he belonged. He went 3–1 in his matches on a team that won 14–10 in Portmarnock, Ireland. But in May's opinion, he had an average college career.

There was something else, though. His coaching throughout his youth focused on positive reinforcement. Well, the cocky young May didn't jive well with Oklahoma State coach Mike Holder riding him. The staff tried to motivate him by pointing out what he *couldn't* do, as if to challenge him. "I didn't react to that kind of coaching. It beat down some of my confidence, totally," he recalled.

He turned professional in 1993 and earned himself a spot on tour in 1994, only to miss twenty-four of thirty-one cuts as his game cratered. He was so far from that cocky kid in Lake Tahoe so sure he could beat anyone. Looking back three decades later, May can see what really happened.

"Any great player in golf, they were cocky. I don't care who it is. They were cocky on the golf course. They might not have been cocky off the course, but they were on it. And I think it's important as an individual, you've got to have a little cock in your walk. If you don't, you're going to get beaten out.

"Some of that was stolen from me in college," he continued.

He'd be hitting balls on a crowded driving range and notice another pro standing behind him waiting. He was taught respect by his elders and let himself respect the other generations too much. May had already waited twenty minutes for that spot, but he'd scoot over to make room for the other pro, forcing himself into a tight little spot. "I should have said, 'No. I earned this spot,'" he says now.

So much of what makes Woods one of the greatest to ever play is that mindset. He is absolutely sure he can and should win any tournament he enters. He is sure he can hit any difficult or creative shot he attempts. When star golfer Curtis Strange interviewed him as he turned pro in 1996, Strange pushed him on the belief that he enters every tournament planning to win, that Woods would need to adjust his expectations when playing the best in the world each week. Woods didn't budge, and Strange infamously scoffed and condescendingly muttered, "You'll learn." When that interview was brought up to May, he said he would have given an identical answer back in his amateur days.

Imagine if Woods' confidence was even slightly diminished. Imagine if he lost any shred of his killer instinct. Woods had so much confidence that he could rework his entire swing, withstand constant scrutiny because he was having a down year, and still be completely sure of himself that it would work out in the long run.

Woods never lost that edge, or at least not until his cheating scandal during Thanksgiving 2009 when the shield of perfectionism was removed. Maybe it started even earlier, when he lost a thrilling 2009 PGA Championship. For what felt like the first time in his career, Woods missed the eight-foot birdie putt that would have kept him tied with Yang. He went on to lose, and Williams called it the first crack in Woods' armor. He later wrote, "It felt like something was ruffling his immaculately honed focus." Three months later his infidelities became international news. Woods remained an elite golfer for another four to five years before the injuries truly wrecked him for good, but the killer faded. As did his major performances. He had lost that unmatched confidence.

One might look back in hindsight and realize it was unprecedented that he maintained it that long.

May is quick to make clear that the Oklahoma State staff made him a better person and a more mature adult. All the coaching that didn't quite work for him also helped him as a human being. He just thinks it cut out his killer instinct in the process.

He continued to grind away overseas, but it wasn't until 1999 that he regained some version of that confidence. Playing on the European Tour, back when many of the best European players stayed there and didn't feel compelled to join the PGA Tour, May had his comeback year. He racked up solid, impressive outings one week after the next to the point contemporaries like Lee Westwood and Darren Clarke playfully called him "Top-10 Bob."

But at the 1999 British Masters, May had himself in the mix. He trailed the great Scotsman Colin Montgomerie by three shots with eighteen holes to go. Monty was the defending champ and had five European wins on the season, one shy of catching Seve Ballesteros' record of six wins in a season. Quickly, May flipped the script from down three to up three on the front nine. May held on to win by one, signifying the true start of the best twelve months in his career.

May then went back to the States to play in the PGA Tour qualifying tournament, where he easily advanced and regained his tour status for 2000. He was back.

At some point that fall, he received a call from a number he didn't know. It was Ballesteros, the beloved five-time major champ.

"Thank you for keeping my record alive," he said.

The other part of the story that gets muddled is the way May was proclaimed a completely out of nowhere story. Sure, in the context of Woods' normal peers on a major Sunday, May was far outside the top tier. But in 2000, he had turned himself into one of the thirty or so best players in the game. In his first ever US Open appearance and second major ever, he finished T23. A month later at the Open, he jumped to T11. And on tour, he was finishing around the top 30 almost every week that summer. In the span of three months, he jumped from 73rd in the Official World Golf Rankings to No. 48 at the PGA Championship.

"Was it David and Goliath compared to Tiger's career? Absolutely," May said. "But was it David and Goliath compared to a normal tour player? No, I don't think it was."

But it meant something to Woods. As much as the story is often told about Woods pinning Nicklaus' long list of achievements to his wall with a mission of surpassing them, the other person on Woods' wall was May. He pinned May's junior golf records to his wall, too, because Woods wanted to overtake May as the best junior in Southern California.

May's father recently found an old photo in storage of May, maybe eleven or twelve, hitting a putt on a California green. Off on the side watching closely were Earl and a toddler version of Tiger Woods. He grew up chasing May, and now May was chasing him.

It was a disgustingly hot August in Kentucky, and all the conversation was around Woods and Nicklaus. The fact that May shot an opening round 72 didn't give anyone reason to pay attention either. Then it rained Thursday night. Valhalla already lacked a reputation as a prestigious major championship venue. The PGA of America, which runs the PGA Championship, owned a majority share of the Nicklaus-designed course and used it often. This was its second PGA Championship at Valhalla since buying shares, and they've hosted two more PGAs, a Ryder Cup, and a Senior PGA Championship in the twenty-five years since.

On one hand, Valhalla always seemed to provide thrilling finishes. The 1996 PGA Championship went to a playoff where Mark Brooks beat Kenny Perry. Then came this duel in 2000 before the 2014 PGA where McIlroy out battled Mickelson and Fowler in a fascinating finish as daylight ran out. In 2024, Xander Schauffele won his first major when he birdied 18 to escape a potential playoff with Bryson DeChambeau.

On the other hand, Valhalla didn't always challenge

the best golfers the way many of the other major venues did. In the eyes of most golf nerds, it was a straightforward, overly simplistic course that didn't inspire much creativity. All four majors held there finished with scores in the double digits under par. So, when the course softened due to Friday's rain, Valhalla lost the one thing protecting it from low scores: its firm greens.

And just before the PGA, veteran Hal Sutton was asked about Woods' domination and warned that Valhalla wasn't set up for him to run away with it the way he did at Pebble and St Andrews. For all of Valhalla's knocks, Sutton said it forced many longer players to hit less off the tee, meaning golfers were all hitting from the same spots from the fairway. It grouped the field together.

"Tiger is a great player," Sutton said. "He plays well every time he goes out . . . But if there is a golf course that is going to neutralize his game a little bit, next week is going to do that somewhat."

May was one of the better iron players in the game, so he was made to attack softer greens. Plus, as much as he looked unassuming at five-foot-seven, May was top 50 on tour in distance. He shot a second-round 66 without a single bogey, as he could aim right at pins. It was an impressive round, pushing May into a tie for sixth, but he was five back of the solo leader, Woods. There was still no reason for anyone to learn May's name.

May wasn't yet thinking about Woods or winning yet. He just knew he had a good thing going. But Saturday, May birdied seven holes in a ten-hole stretch to shoot yet another 66. So, when Scott Dunlap failed to birdie 18 in the final group, it sealed the deal that May would play in the final group, trailing Woods by one shot.

At that moment, May thought of all the greats who've played against Tiger on the final day and faltered. He thought of the Sunday red shirt and the effect it can have. He didn't sleep great that night, but one mantra kept going through his mind, his key to surviving against the best in the world: *You and Tiger are going to play a different golf course tomorrow. The way he can play it is different from how I can play it. I can't get into a slugfest with him. I have to do it a different way.*

To contend with Tiger Woods, he couldn't try to be somebody else. He had to believe in his own game. Fortunately for him, he had a little cock in his walk.

Chapter Nine

ON THE ROPES

Tiger Woods was used to arriving at tournaments to play the final round in the final group. He was used to pulling up in his courtesy car with cameras waiting. Used to fans lining the area begging for autographs. He'd done it so many times, and that Sunday was no different. He hopped out of the car at Valhalla in a dark red Nike polo with a black collar. He wore a sleek, modern set of matrix sunglasses. Somebody grabbed his bags. Another official approached him with where to go. He walked by without noticing his surroundings, because this was all a scene he'd lived before. He looked like the 2000 version of the biggest star in sports that he was.

Then, May arrived at the club in his red rental car. He hopped out without much fanfare. He opened his trunk and pulled out his own white golf bag. When he started to walk, he noticed the camera and gave a dad-like wave and smile.

Never had the contrast felt starker on a major Sunday.

They went to the first tee, where May kept to his mantra for the day. He hit a normal, successful drive down the right side of the fairway on the dogleg left sitting at the base of a massive sixty-foot tree. He felt good about it. Until Woods went up and smashed a ball that May actually thought Woods pulled. No, Woods just cut the corner so well that his ball flew over the same sixty-foot tree and left himself a short wedge in.

"Right off the bat it's verified," May said. "We're going to play a different golf course today."

May is and was a student of the game, though. He loved studying history and the different ways different players handled certain moments. He loved deploying psychological tricks or what could get a player off their plan. Would any of that work on Woods? Probably not. But one thing he liked was that *because* he was shorter, it meant May would usually hit first into the greens. Well, May took immense pride in his iron game.

"If I could keep on hitting good shots into the green, he has to see that," May said.

They both parred that first hole, but Woods made a mess of No. 2 including a poor chip. Woods bogeyed while May made a birdie, immediately flipping the leaderboard for a solo May lead. Then, on 4, he hit from thick rough and placed a beautiful shot that landed just over a large bunker and rolled to the pin for birdie. In a matter of minutes, May went from down one to leading Woods by two at the PGA Championship.

Suddenly, May could breathe. And Woods got his poor start out of the way. They both made mistakes on No. 6 for bogey, but from there on out, they played one of the great Sunday duels in recent memory. Woods wasn't quite his dominant self that he was at the previous two majors. He wasn't sinking the exceptional number of putts, but he was still playing solid Tiger Woods golf, enough to win most events handily. Normally, Williams would watch as the Tiger Effect went into place and whoever was in the mix with Woods faded away.

"Except this time, Bob wasn't buying into the fear factor," Williams said. "It was one of the few times during Tiger's dominant years when he met a rival who not only stood up to him but played better for most of the day."

———

The history of Tiger Woods on Sundays goes so much deeper than you may know.

It's well known that Woods was the first to win the U.S. Junior Amateur three years in a row, and he was the first to win the U.S. Amateur three years in a row, as well. But the other part of those stories is that each and every one went down to the final hole.

All of Woods' majors up to this point were blowouts. That was not a knock. That was a testament to his ability. But the wider golf game hadn't seen him play down to the wire with everything on the line. They wanted to see Woods coming up clutch under pressure like Nicklaus always did.

Harmon, though, knew that was actually where Woods did his best work.

"He always had that ability to pull the greatness out of himself," Harmon said of a young Woods playing in amateurs. "I'm not sure he knew how he was going to do it, but he knew he was going to do it."

First, in the 1991 U.S. Junior at Bay Hill, Woods tried to become the youngest junior champion in history at fifteen. Playing the sixteen-year-old Brad Zwetschke, it went to a playoff when Woods bogeyed the 18th hole. There, Zwetschke double bogeyed to give Woods the win.

The next year, he trailed Mark Wilson by two shots with five holes to go in the final. Woods had to get hot, and won 14 and 16 to level Wilson with two to go. Wilson kept leaving Woods in pressure situations to make tough 50–50 putts, and Woods wouldn't break. He chipped away and chipped away until 18, when Wilson collapsed and Woods became the first two-time winner of the U.S. Junior.

He went for the three-peat in Oregon, where he faced future tour pro Ryan Armour. More than five thousand people surrounded these teenagers, and Woods launched drives over trees that left approaches eighty yards shorter than Armour had to hit. He exhausted Armour, and by the time they reached a playoff, Armour hit it over the green and Woods won with a safe par.

Next was a mission to beat Nicklaus' record as the youngest U.S. Amateur champ. Nicklaus won it as a nineteen-year-old Ohio State junior. Woods was eighteen and still in high school. He advanced to the final, where he reached a problem. Playing at TPC Sawgrass, he trailed the twenty-two-year-old Oklahoma State All-American Trip Kuehne by six holes with thirteen to go.

Kuehne came from money, the son of an oil company CEO who trained with well-known coach Hank Haney from a young age. They were friends, but Kuehne and Woods came from two different worlds. It made Woods want it even more. But nobody had ever come back from a six-hole deficit to win the U.S. Amateur. First, he just wanted to get it to two or three by the turn. He slowly chipped away at his lead, and by seventeen they were even.

No. 17 at Sawgrass is known as the most intimidating par 3 in the world. It's short, but it is a tiny green alone on an island surrounded by water on all sides. The only connection to land is a tiny, thin path behind it. It messes with the minds of the best pros, and Woods was eighteen chasing history. He hit a wedge that, in his mind, "should have gone in the water," but it bounced off the fringe and somehow stayed. Woods hit his putt from the fringe, but it clearly hit something and kicked slightly farther up the slope. Woods laughed retelling it, as the bounce fixed his misread putt and fell for birdie.

As it went in, Woods hopped to his left and lunged while making a dramatic, swooping fist pump. His fist circled from well below his waist and up above his head while shouting, "Yeah!" He couldn't stop celebrating. He kept pumping his fist as he walked over to the hole. It was the early sign of a celebration that would follow Woods forever, and he did it to become the youngest—and first Black—U.S. Amateur in history.

His next victim was George "Buddy" Marucci, a forty-three-year-old Mercedes-Benz dealer who might not have hit it far but put it right down the center of the fairway every drive. Marucci led through the first 18, but Woods hit a lengthy putt on 17 to take the lead to the final hole. He'd been working with Harmon at this point for two years, and one thing Harmon worked with him on for playing Newport Country Club was a knockdown shot to fight through the wind. He insisted Woods would need it. And on 18, with 140 yards to the hole, Woods called for an 8-iron to attempt that knockdown shot. He hit a shot that landed well past the hole and spun back to just a foot from the hole to seal a second consecutive U.S. Amateur.

And Woods' final amateur event was at Pumpkin Ridge in 1996, trying to become the first ever three-time champ. At this point, Woods was a national star. He already had a handshake deal with Nike, and Nike founder Phil Knight even made the trip. Anticipation was building that Woods would turn professional after the week, but Woods had business first.

Woods had won thirty consecutive matches leading up

to the final with Florida sophomore Steve Scott, but through eighteen holes he trailed by five. Here was a U.S. Amateur with more coverage than any before it because of Woods, and he was going to lose. Harmon saw what was wrong.

"It was all posture related," Harmon said. "His posture was bad. He didn't even go to lunch. We went and fixed it. Then he went right out."

Woods fired back to get it within one shot, and the back nine turned into a back-and-forth contest. Scott chipped in from heavy rough on 10. Then Woods made a thirty-five-foot putt with a large break for eagle. When they went to 16, Scott led by two. Woods put his approach to six feet, surely in good position, but when Scott asked him to move his ball marker because it was in his line, Woods forgot to put it back where it was. He needed to make this putt to win the hole, and Scott was the only one who noticed Woods was about to hit from the wrong spot. That would cost Woods the hole. Scott, out of good sportsmanship, jumped in to ask Woods if he moved his ball back. He hadn't, and Woods realized and moved the ball back. If Scott hadn't told him, he would have won the U.S. Amateur right there. Instead, Woods won the hole with his birdie putt.

Twenty years later, Woods said of the incident: "I did forget [to move my ball back]. For him to [remind me] was pretty remarkable. Ever since that one moment I always mark my marker heads up, and if I ever move my coin or someone asks me to move it, I always move it to tails, so when I look down at my ball if it's showing tails, that means I moved it. That's true sportsmanship [what Scott did]. A testament to what the game of golf is all about."

Woods birdied 17 to level the match, and they ultimately went to yet another sudden death playoff where on the second hole Scott missed his par putt to give Woods his third straight U.S. Amateur.

Shortly after, he turned pro as a man well-seasoned for Sunday golf.

———

May and Woods talked and got along well for much of that front nine. There wasn't much tension at all. Woods birdied 7 and 8 to bring it level at 13-under as they went to the back nine, but still May refused to look at the leaderboard. Not once. But what history forgets is how close the pack remained. At that moment, five other golfers (seven total) remained within three shots of the lead. Thomas Bjorn, Stuart Appleby, Greg Chalmers, and Franklin Langham all got to 12-under. But when Woods and May went to the turn, that was when May truly found his game and became the major competitor he was always supposed to be. That was also when the chitchat ended. That's when it became about two Southern California boys going for the title.

They both birdied the par 5 No. 10, but May somehow made a long, fast-running birdie putt across the large green for birdie on 11 while Woods "settled" for an easier birdie. The crowd roared for May. Yes, the crowd still certainly pulled for Woods, but they were beginning to root for May, too. Then, on 12, May hit a perfect iron shot to within five feet for birdie—his third birdie in a row—when Woods hit a difficult twenty-foot birdie to keep within pace. May was hot, and he had a one-shot lead, but these two kept exchanging haymakers each hole.

The closer you looked into Woods' eyes throughout that round, the more the robotic veneer faded away. The more you could see enjoyment, Woods relishing a true contest for a major championship. When he missed a tough, winding birdie putt on 13, he dropped to a pained squat and then smiled with his tongue out to the side. He walked to finish his par putt and took off his hat, mouthing "fuck" on the way. He knew he couldn't miss those opportunities when May didn't score.

May still wasn't looking at the leaderboard, but he noticed more and more people focused on their group. He began to figure it was all about them. On the par 3 No. 14, May hit a beautiful, controlled fade that bounced just over the steep bunker and rolled right to the pin. It was perfect. Woods, again reminding May they played a different course, hit a completely different shot. He went long to the back left corner of the green and spun it back to the center just a few feet from May's ball. They both made their putts for birdie, May remaining one ahead.

But it was when they walked down from that 14th tee shot, down the stairs and across the creek in the middle of the hole, that Woods noticed a hospitality tent to the left. The crowd of course roared "Tiger! Tiger! Tiger!" on repeat. Until one disproportionately loud voice interjected.

"What about Bob!?" the voice shouted, referencing the 1991 Bill Murray film.

May finally laughed, and the crowd only roared more with him once they saw him break. He felt the tide shifting in that moment. They weren't against Tiger. But they fully wanted to see a great match. "Before, I think everybody just wanted to see Tiger dominate," he recalled.

On 15, Valhalla has a large body of water guarding the green along the front and right sides. On Sunday, they tucked the pin in the front right, putting the water even more in play. Any sane person would either fade it where it stayed over land or just aim well past the pin for safety, like Woods did.

But May pulled out a 7-iron and went bold. He hit the ball over the water, drawing it back toward the pin. The man had a lead at the PGA Championship, and it carried so much risk to even try this in the moment, yet May stuck it four feet from the pin. Woods looked back and saw Williams just shake his head. This guy wouldn't go away.

"Nobody really understood the shot he hit," Woods said after the round with a reverent smile. "With the water there, to step up there and hit the ball, what, eight yards right of the hole and draw it back in? It's pretty impressive."

Here was a chance for a two-shot swing. Woods missed the green while May was putting for birdie. May had a chance for a three-shot lead if all went right. Woods left his chip a good distance from the hole for par. He later called that par putt the most important shot of the day, but he made it, putting the pressure back on May.

To this day, May maintains he didn't mishit the putt. He thinks he read it correctly. "Olazábal had the exact same putt and it broke right," May said. "I just hit a putt that didn't break." The short putt ran right past the hole, leaving his most impressive shot of the day unrewarded. Instead of a three-shot lead, they went to 16 with May's lead still one. They parred that, too.

May missed the fairway on 17 and would have to settle for a safe two-putt par. Here was Woods' chance as he sat in the fairway.

"What have we got, Stevie?" Woods asked.

Williams measured ninety-five yards to the hole, but for at least the second time in a major that year he decided to lie to the best player in the world. He'd been around long enough to know that sometimes, late in these tournaments, Woods would get too amped up. Without even knowing it, his adrenaline rose to the point that his shots kept going longer and longer. Williams knew that if he told Woods the truth, ninety-five yards, Woods would ask for a sand wedge. But Williams worried he'd fly a sand wedge too far. It would have been an argument at the crucial moment trailing by one. So he told him ninety yards.

"Lob wedge," Woods responded.

With a bunker guarding the tucked pin, Woods hit it perfectly over the bunker and spun it to two feet from the hole for birdie. The PGA Championship was tied.

On 18, a winding par 5, both had eagle putts from a distance, and both missed. But May let his fly by. He had to get it up a four-foot hill on the green and put way too much on it, rolling well past the hole and onto the fringe. *I cannot believe I just hit that putt at this point in my career*, he thought. And for the first time all day, May let himself look up at the leaderboard. He saw they were four shots ahead and putting for birdie. It was just between them.

His only mission on that putt was to not leave it short. And when he hit it, he was sure it was short. Again, he couldn't believe it. But it kept going, and the double breaker went left to right and back left into the cup. May launched a fist pump high into the air with a one-shot lead and Woods needing to make a downhill eight-footer for a playoff.

Williams maintains he saw May prepare to shake his hand before the putt, as if to imply May thought Woods would miss. "I could read the look on his face," Williams said. "It was full of anticipation that said, 'I'm going to win the PGA.'" May, on the other hand, is adamant he always thought Woods would make it. But what he will admit is standing on the green was the first time he ever let himself think that maybe, just maybe, he could win the PGA Championship.

But Woods made the challenging putt, letting out an

animal yell to the Kentucky crowd as he forced the playoff. Williams asked Woods what he was thinking on the putt.

"Stevie, my mom could've made that putt," Woods said. "I'm Tiger Woods. I'm supposed to make that putt. It ain't no big deal, Stevie."

So, on the back nine of the PGA Championship final round, both Woods and May shot 31. May shot a third-consecutive 66 to go from 72 to in the playoff with Woods. They shook hands, Woods grinning ear to ear. Tournament officials sent Woods to one side of the media and May to another, and Ken Venturi kept going off to May about how this was the most special golf duel ever played. May didn't get it. He was so in the moment that the gravity of the situation still escaped him. He even had the wherewithal to say no, he thought the best ever was Nicklaus vs. Isao Aoki in the 1980 US Open.

"I spent most of the week on the golf course," commentator David Feherty said, "and the final nine holes on Sunday were the most compelling golf I'd ever seen."

There was almost no break between 18 and the playoff. Until that year, the PGA always went to a sudden death playoff, so May assumed they would go back to the 18th tee. But this was the first year of a new three-hole aggregate playoff format replaying 16-17-18.

"I remember that we were informed it was a three-hole playoff and Bob was completely shocked by that," Woods said, "because I don't think that it really got out that much that potentially it could be the way it plays out."

It was the first time May started thinking too far ahead. He admits it threw him off. He was tired, as was Woods, but May let that surprise show. Maybe right then Woods had the mental advantage.

On 16, May missed the fairway and left himself in more trouble on the recovery. He hit a nice pitch on his third shot that nearly holed out, but he settled for par while Woods had a long putt for birdie.

But Woods turned that long putt into one of the most iconic images of his career. The putt was still five feet from the cup, and Woods took off. He started to strut toward the hole. Three big galloping paces and the ball still wasn't there. But he was sure. He was halfway there before it sunk in. It was one of the most aggressive moves anyone had seen on a golf course, with Woods pointing his finger at the cup as he walked it in. He never stopped his stride, picking the ball up and running off to 17 while continuing to yell and stride. The crowd erupted. It was like it was over right then and there.

May didn't mind the bold display. That's golf.

"The only thing I mind is that for the last twenty years, every time I play a Pro-Am all these guys mimic that and I go, 'Do you guys know the tournament he did that at?'"

And as if this tournament couldn't take on any more drama, the third playoff hole added more controversy. Woods still led by one, and his drive on 18 flew way left and into the gallery. The CBS cameras briefly lost track of the ball, but after a few moments, the ball came flying out, seemingly in the other direction, with plenty of speed.

It was a strange visual. And only adding to the case was the sight of one young man running down the hill—seemingly with nobody else nearby—before the ball took off.

"What happened with that ball?" Venturi asked on the broadcast.

"Do you think someone either kicked it or threw it back in that direction?" Jim Nantz countered.

"I don't know. It, it didn't . . ."

"It didn't react naturally, did it?"

"No, it didn't at all."

"I sure hope someone didn't slap it back," Nantz said.

"It could have been someone jumped up and hit it with their hand."

Because of this bizarre roll, Woods had a solid lie and could lay up back into play. He was able to save par, and

May missed his birdie opportunity, giving Woods his third major title in a row and fourth in five major starts. He became the first golfer since Hogan to win three majors in a year, let alone three in a row.

But that first shot became a conspiracy theory that's existed for decades. May received a fifty-gallon trash bag worth of letters from people convinced they saw something with the boy hitting or kicking the ball. The letters became so constant that they finally had to have an attorney write one man to stop sending letters because it was bordering on harassment.

The shot became a pet project for *Golf Digest* reporter Joel Beall. He spoke to as many people there that day as he could. Some were adamant that they saw something happen. Others said it trickled down the hill. But after his story ran diving into the conspiracy, the boy—now a man—in white running near the ball reached out. He said the ball bounced off the cart path, hitting some low branches and then dropping to the dirt on the top of that hill, where the ball very slowly rolled down the hill and picked up speed before hitting the cart path again and bouncing quickly away.

We may never know what really happened, but May brushes it off. He thinks if something suspicious really happened, somebody would have come forward by now.

All that mattered in the moment was that Woods won the Wanamaker Trophy, continuing his epic campaign for the history books. It was becoming harder and harder to brush off any element of what Woods achieved. Even if his run ended with those three major wins, most would argue it was already the greatest season in history. Even Nicklaus, the man constantly reminding people his era was harder, conceded defeat after the win.

"I kept saying, 'I can't understand why we don't have anybody else playing that well,'" Nicklaus said after his two rounds with Woods. "I am more understanding now. He's that much better."

May hung around for a few more years. He proved he belonged on the PGA Tour and that he wasn't just some flavor of the week. Until May's back gave out and he underwent surgery before the 2004 season, he steadily made cuts and kept his card. It took him away from the game for years, and he never quite regained his level.

May looks back on that PGA Championship now with nothing but joy. He was always raised to believe golf was about beating the golf course, not the opponents, and he could sleep at night knowing both he and Woods beat the golf course that day. He takes solace in the fact that few look at it as May losing as much as Woods winning. But even more than all of that, he's not sure winning would have made his life better. Sure, he would have earned more tour exemptions and money. He likely would have earned some more endorsements, too. But he's quite confident he'll be remembered more for losing that duel during the greatest season ever than if he would have won it.

Every year from 2000 to 2022, May still got calls about the face-off and always obliged. He loves talking about that moment and giving back. In 2023, he realized it was the first time nobody called. That was made up for by 2024, when the PGA returned to Valhalla and authors worked on books about the Tiger Slam.

But that day back in August 2000, he took Tiger Woods to the brink. And after all the media hoopla and the celebration, Woods made his way to the parking lot. As the walk continued, Woods finally stopped hiding his limp. He groaned about his calf killing him. He finally sat down in his car ready to be driven away and told a reporter, "Man, I'm tired. It's been a long day."

It was not the other top ten stars of the tour and former major winners who finally made Tiger Woods bleed at his peak.

No, it was Bob May.

———

Chapter Ten

THE ANTICIPATION

There's a major character in this book you haven't heard from in quite a while. The golf world thought the same thing at the time. Through much of the 1990s, you couldn't read a golf story without a long, interesting, chaotic quote from Earl Woods. That's because he was everywhere. He managed Tiger's career. He led his foundation. He went to what felt like most tournaments and gave his thoughts to any reporter with a microphone. He was the man who proudly took the title of architect of the greatest athlete in the world. He wrote books. Books were written about him.

But by 2000, Earl didn't show up to tournaments. When he did, he couldn't walk the course and remained hidden. An absence that large was noticed, but in those days reporters on the beat every day didn't want to dig up dirt to hurt their relationship with Woods and his team. The conflict with that was that Woods didn't give much to the media anyway.

For one, Earl's health was in decline. He ultimately lived until 2006, but by April 2000 *Sports Illustrated* already wrote he was "courting death." He was severely overweight, had three open-heart surgeries, and had just beaten a bout with prostate cancer, yet he showed zero interest in changing his health habits. He still ate poorly and refused to curb his cigarette smoking. "I know smoking is wrong, but I contend there's no cholesterol in a cigarette," he said. "Tiger doesn't like it, but he's accepted that I'm just like him: stubborn as hell." He was sixty-eight, often fading to sleep when sitting in his chair or running out of breath.

"He said, 'This is the way I want to live my life,'" Kultida said. "But I want to see my son's future. I want to see my grandkids. Dad wants to check out first? Fine with me. But I want to stay longer."

As much as Earl said Tiger accepted it, the way Earl

handled his health frustrated Tiger, who often nagged him to cut out smoking. He revered his father, calling him his "best friend," and that friend was fading away.

In the summer of 2000, Earl told another reporter, "I'm not ready to die, if that's what you mean. I don't go to the tournaments anymore because I get mobbed and can't see any golf."

In another interview, he implied this was all his plan: "I raised Tiger to leave me."

Earl and Tiger steadily pushed reasons like this for why Earl wasn't around as much, but it was more complicated than that. By 2000, Tiger was twenty-four. To Earl's point, Tiger had grown into his own man, and that showed in many of his actions around that time. Keep in mind, that stretch from 1998 to 2000 was a time of change for Woods as he created his *own* life. His entire adolescence was planned by Earl. When he turned professional in 1996, each step of his career and his never-ending list of endorsement obligations were scheduled by Earl and agent Hughes Norton. Look at the other changes in Tiger's life, and there's a theme. He moved on from Norton as his commitments became too much, wanting to focus more on golf, shortly after Norton shared a *Golf World* cover with Tiger and Earl titled "The Father, Son, and Holy Ghost."

He parted ways with Fluff Cowan in part because Cowan was taking on too much attention in his own right. He replaced all these figures with people like Sternberg and Williams who kept a lower profile. He also had a serious girlfriend, Joanna Jagoda, who by all accounts grounded Woods' life at the time.

And for better or worse, Earl fit into that category of a larger-than-life figure adding distractions away from golf.

At this point, Earl and Kultida were separated and living in different houses. His infidelity to Kultida was hardly a secret, and Woods was well aware by then. According to the Keteyian and Benedict biography, Earl stopped even trying to hide his vices. He brought a younger woman to the 1998 Presidents Cup and by 2000 filled the house with different women in and out.

Woods always protected his father publicly, though. He didn't hide the growing distance, but he chalked it up to a son growing on his own. He did admit he didn't always have time for Earl's calls. "My dad and I don't talk as much," he said. "He's doing his thing. I'm doing my thing."

In a *Sports Illustrated* piece early in that 2000 season, Earl said, "We don't have to communicate with each other to validate our relationship. I don't have to say 'Oh, Tiger, I love you.' Are you kidding me? I haven't talked to Tiger in two weeks, and he was in Los Angeles and San Diego. No big deal."

To Earl, they could speak without speaking. He loved to tell the story of Woods standing over his difficult par putt at the 1999 PGA Championship in the battle against García. As Woods lined up, Earl said he spoke to him through a hotel TV in Chicago: *Tiger. This is a must-make putt. Trust your stroke. Trust your stroke.* Tiger made the putt, and when they met later that night, Woods told him, "I heard you, Pop." When Woods made his difficult birdie putt on 18 at Valhalla to send it to a playoff, Rick Reilly watched with Earl and heard him mutter again under his breath, "Trust it, Tiger. Trust your stroke." While all these stories feel like folklore, nobody could deny the depth of their bond.

When a reporter asked Tiger about the distance, he added, "When I first turned pro, he was always there for me, we could talk at night. Then as I began to understand what it took to play out here and the obligations that come with being a professional golfer, he gradually did what most parents do: let their child go. He's always there for guidance when asked. He may observe from the outside and may offer a suggestion every now and then. But he has never said, 'You really need to do this.' Now I do whatever I want to do."

Because the other part of Woods' evolution from 1998 to 2000—the swing, the caddie, the agent, the family dynamics—is the removal of sentimentality as Woods became a true killer on and off the course. Sure, he got better at dealing with the media and other players. He cut back on the angry tirades. He was a more well-rounded public figure. But even those actions were as much about removing any and all controversy from his life.

From then on, everything was about maximizing what he could become. That part, it appeared, didn't include Earl.

"He's more like Mom," Kultida said. "When I say 'enough,' don't ever come ask me again. I cut and move on. Tiger's more like me."

———

Notah Begay III called Woods the Monday morning after the PGA Championship. It was a late night after a three-hole playoff and surely some celebration, so Woods' old Stanford golf teammate Begay checked in to see what he was up to.

"I'm on the driving range practicing."

Begay couldn't comprehend this. He just won his third

major in a row. He was in the middle of the best season of all time, and the night before was the most exhausting round of them all.

For the most part, though, Woods took two days off. By Wednesday, he had to be in Akron, Ohio, for the WGC-NEC Invitational at Firestone Country Club, one of four World Golf Championships played each year back then. It's easy to focus on the majors, especially in 2025 as a fractured golf world makes majors feel like the only events that matter, but what took Woods' year to an extra level nobody will catch are the ten wins worldwide. There was never just some hot streak or a nice few months in major season. He won in January, February, March, May, June, July, August, and September. He finished worse than 11th just twice, and those were 18th- and 23rd-place finishes.

Less than four days removed from a playoff win, he took the first-round lead in Akron at 6-under. It was only a one-shot lead. Disappointing. A second round 61 immediately took that lead to seven shots. His domination became such a joke that reporters asked players after the second round if a tournament could be over by Friday when it came to Woods. They did not like that.

"A little disappointing you would even bring that up," said Mickelson in second place.

The next day, that lead grew to nine. More questions for Mickelson.

"Again," he said, "I think that people watching on television or yourself or other people asking these questions are looking at it in how I stand in relation to the leader, and that's not how I'm looking at it."

Of course, the tournament was going to end in another Woods victory, but the reason this event lives on is how he won it. Storms earlier in the day delayed the final round, and it became a race to get the finish in before sunset. As Woods approached his ball on the first cut of rough on 18, it was so dark he had to squat down and get close to the ball just to see his lie. He could barely make out the flagstick 168 yards away. Fog didn't help the situation either.

No, none of this truly mattered. He led by ten shots. "True, I had a big lead," Woods said, "but I wanted to close things out in style." He took out an 8-iron and hacked a few practice swings to get a feel for the ground in relation to the club. The turf was firm, making him confident he could hit it a normal 8-iron distance.

It's a common reference on a late-night golf broadcast that the course might be darker than it appears on TV because the cameras have their irises all the way open to get any and all light. It's true. The broadcast during McIlroy's win at the 2014 PGA Championship looks far brighter on TV than the reality. But in Akron, it looked pitch black even on TV. Fans in the gallery held up cigarette lighters to try helping like it was a rock concert.

This moment—Tiger Woods hitting a completely blind shot to seal a golf tournament—perfectly tells the story of 2000. Other than maybe Bob May, Woods was playing a sport of his own. The only thing that could keep him from another win was Mother Nature. He relished it, though. He and Earl used to sneak on the Navy Course and try to get a few holes in before dark.

He immediately lost the ball to the dark as it shot into the air. He waited and waited, having no idea where it would land, only learning his fate when the Akron crowd erupted. The ball landed two feet from the hole and Nantz shouted, "You can't do that!" on the CBS broadcast as Woods high-fived Williams to say, "How 'bout that?" He tapped in his putt and won by eleven shots. He also became the first player since Johnny Miller in 1975 to successfully defend three different titles in the same year, winning the PGA Championship, the Memorial, and Firestone in consecutive years.

We found out later that Woods and Williams had a running battle to get to 21-under all year. It was Williams' favorite number, and they fell just shy at the Memorial at 19-under. Same for St Andrews. So, on the final hole, as Woods asked for a new glove because his was getting a little wet, Williams wrote "21" on the glove.

Just another example of Woods creating mini competitions in a blowout.

"[Steve] was so excited," Woods joked. "I mean, I've won major championships, and he was not that excited. And I guess I finally got to his favorite number."

But while Woods thinks back to his St Andrews shot as his best in 2000, most say it was a shot he hit two weeks later in the Canadian Open.

Woods was in a Sunday duel with thirty-six-year-old New Zealander Grant Waite. He couldn't shake him, trading birdies all day until Woods led by one on 18, a 508-yard par 5. It was once again getting dark, this time with rain, when Woods hit his drive into a bunker on the right side of the fairway. Waite had no issue putting his second shot onto the green to leave himself a long putt for eagle, most likely two-putting for birdie. If Woods wanted to win it right there, he'd likely have to birdie from the bunker. "It really forced my hand," Woods said. "Instead of taking a shorter club and aiming for the middle of the green, I had to take one more club and try to hit it close."

Nobody went for the back right pin from the right side of the fairway on 18, let alone the bunker. There was a big oak tree in his line, water guarding everything in front and right of the green and a bunker right behind the pin. Plus, the wind was blowing right toward the water. The landing zone was minuscule. But Woods set up a line to attack. Media members lost their minds. Waite was shocked.

Woods had been working on a new fairway bunker technique he discovered back home at Isleworth. It consisted of flattening his swing plane slightly in order to shallow out his approach angle into the ball. He believed it left more margin for error. Then he weakened his grip to ensure he wouldn't turn the clubface over.

He ripped it, and immediately the broadcast thought he pushed it too far right to the water. But no, it was right on line toward the pin. It hit the back of the green, two feet behind the pin, and took one bounce before settling just along the fringe to leave himself an easy birdie for the win.

"That one shot I did hit, it was pretty good," Woods said, "but you know what? I didn't hit the green. I hit it over the green, so it wasn't really that good."

It gave Woods his tenth worldwide win and ninth of the PGA Tour season. It also made him the first golfer since Lee Trevino in 1971 to win all of the main national opens—US Open, British Open, and Canadian Open—in the same year. Every week another historic shot. Every week a new historic milestone.

Later after all the festivities, Williams walked back on his own to the bunker. He wanted to get another look at what his employer did, to understand the focus and talent it took to execute that shot.

Scott Verplank called it the best shot he'd ever seen in his life.

———

One of the most dangerous things about reaching the level Woods had is that it made the masses lose any rational perception of what's normal. All expectations for the average No. 1 player were thrown away. And when a golfer became such a crossover megastar like Woods, it also meant more and more eyeballs that weren't used to the usual ways a golf season unfolds.

Golf is by nature a sport built for variance. It is not constructed to allow domination, even by somebody who is, by all accounts, dominant. It is a sport where 100 to 150 people play seventy-two holes over four days, where the gap between the top twenty players might be five to ten shots. In your average season going into a marquee event like the Players Championship, the betting favorite *might* have a 7 percent probability of winning. The tenth best player in the world might have a 3 percent probability. During his historically dominant 2024 campaign, Scottie Scheffler reached the highest betting odds since prime Tiger, and those 4-to-1 odds implied a 20 percent probability. And it is perhaps the sport where form is the most volatile. A nice run may last three weeks tops.

The best players in the world historically play somewhere between twenty and thirty tournaments a year. During the agreed-upon best golf season of all time, Woods won a comical ten of twenty-one starts. If you scroll through every PGA Tour season of the last few decades, the overwhelming majority include the "player of the year" winning three, four, or in extremely rare occasions five tournaments a season.

It is a game where golfers should not be judged by wins but by overall performance week to week. Scheffler won just two tournaments in 2023, yet nobody came close to approaching him for world No. 1 because he finished top 5 at an absurd rate. Two-time major winner Collin Morikawa didn't win a single tournament in 2024. He finished the year ranked No. 4 in the world, because he racked up fourteen top-20s and seven top-5s.

No golfer is ever *supposed* to win.

All of this to help contextualize the stage for the weekly defamation that became "The Tiger Slump" of 2001.

After winning in Canada, Woods ended his legendary 2000 campaign by finishing 3, 2, T5 at the final three events. That included Mickelson edging him out for the Tour Championship, a nice feather in Mickelson's cap to round out a fantastic four-win season as world No. 2. He was named *Sports Illustrated*'s Sportsman of the Year, the first athlete to ever earn the honor twice. His endorsements continued to explode. But after what Woods did in 2000, any loss was starting to be treated as Woods failing.

His form certainly didn't dip as 2001 came around. He finished T8 at the Mercedes Championship in Kapalua. He finished T5 at the Phoenix Open. At Pebble Beach it was T13 (horrible, right?), and at the Buick Invitational at Torrey Pines he finished solo fourth. Mickelson won that one, too. It was around then that the word "slump" started to be thrown around. Pay no mind to the fact that his scoring average was actually better in 2001 than his illustrious 2000, something Woods was quick to remind anybody asking him about his lack of wins.

At first, his responses were on the more playful side. The questions irked him, but he could play it off with sarcasm.

"It's not a slump," Woods said the day before the Buick. "If I can go [six] tournaments without a victory and people call it a slump, then it must mean I've played some pretty good golf."

After coming up short at the Buick, he finished T13 at the Nissan Open at Riviera, a course Woods was for whatever reason never able to conquer, ironic considering it is now the event he hosts each year.

Remember Jimmy Roberts, the NBC reporter who got on Woods' bad side for asking about his expletives at Pebble Beach? The week before the Bay Hill Invitational, he did a piece for NBC essentially defending Woods, playfully saying that it was the equivalent of the Beatles going a few months without a No. 1 record. Woods didn't quite take it as a defense. All he heard was another reporter using the word "slump."

The week of the Bay Hill Invitational, a reporter tried to get Woods to open up about it, asking him how much the slump talk bothered him.

"Well, it's annoying because of the fact that if you think that way, then you really don't understand the game of golf," Woods said before the tournament began, mentioning that he was 75-under par for the year. "That's not playing bad. I just didn't win. That's part of the game. I try sometimes and it works out. Sometimes it doesn't."

When Roberts asked him about it, he also implied that he didn't understand golf either. The challenge was that Woods was, in fact, right, but he was also taking it out on the wrong people. Woods just won one tournament between 1997 and his 1999 breakout. Was that a slump? He'd gone eight tournaments without a win entering the week. In 2000, he never went more than three.

Woods won in Bay Hill, ending the so-called slump, and he did it without playing very good golf. "That's the beauty of our game," he said. "It's very fickle. That's one of the reasons why we all love to play it because there are days when you go out there and you play great. Other days, you play great and you score like a dog." His next start, he went to the Players Championship—the biggest non-major on tour—and edged out Singh by one shot to take the Players for the first time. Per usual, he did an immediate post-round interview for NBC with Roberts. Guess how that went.

As Roberts attempted to ask a question, Woods ignored him and muttered, "Some slump."

Roberts tried asking something else. Woods again ignored him. "Means the slump is over."

Again, Roberts tried to keep the interview going, and Woods walked away in the middle of a question, leaving Roberts in the lurch on live TV.

Woods was in a less sassy mood when he made his way to the media center, ready to celebrate his win. But the first question was about that awkward interaction with Roberts. The reporter asked if he was just having fun with Roberts as he mocked the slump talk or was he truly sick of this?

"I was," Woods said. "Some of the writers—and I know who they are, had suggested and said it. Obviously, they don't really understand the game that well, because if you look at the way I was playing, I wasn't playing that bad. It wasn't like I was missing cuts every week. I was right there with a chance to win in virtually every tournament I teed up in, and I think that's pretty good. It's just that I had not won, and that's part of the game. It is a game that's very fickle. You can try as hard as you want, and sometimes it just doesn't work out. Now I've won two tournaments in a row, and I'm sure they will write about something else."

The slump talk ended there, but secretly that slump discussion may have temporarily taken attention from the other conversation that was going to permeate that spring: the Grand Slam.

Everywhere he went, some iteration of the same question followed him. "In your mind, would it be the Grand Slam?" "Do you consider the Grand Slam all in one year?" It left Woods in a difficult spot. For starters, he hadn't even won the 2001 Masters yet, so answering these questions directly would look like he was predicting he'd win. Then, for all of his epic run, he successfully avoided these questions by saying his only goal was winning the tournament. What the win would mean could come at another time. But he also couldn't lie to himself. He was one of the most competitive humans to walk this Earth. He brought up the Grand Slam to O'Meara as early as 1997 before he played a single professional major. Of course he wanted it.

As for what qualified the achievement? He had a simple sentiment: Call it what you want.

"Obviously I'm not going to deny this. It is probably the hardest—it is the harder way to accomplish a Grand Slam in one year," he said two days before the Masters. "There's no doubt about that. But I think if you can put all four trophies on your coffee table, I think you can make a pretty good case for that, too."

Of course, the all-time greats had microphones in front of them asking their thoughts on the matter. All of them honored Woods but poo-pooed any discussion of a Grand Slam.

"If Tiger wins, he is starting a new season," said Arnold Palmer, the partial creator of the professional slam. "It's not a continuation of last year."

"You know winning a Grand Slam is winning all four of them in one year," Jack Nicklaus said. "What is your year—fiscal or calendar?"

"I don't see how you can give him a mulligan," Gary Player said. "He didn't win this event last year."

Hootie Johnson, the then-chairman of Augusta National, put it this way: "If Tiger Woods wins this tournament, it will be the greatest achievement in modern day golf. I think we are talking too much about what it will not be, as opposed to what it will be if he does."

In these discussions is a reminder of the absurdity of the fact that this felt inevitable. For all the earlier conversation about how hard it is to win a golf tournament and the low percentages of any man in the field, Woods winning the 2001 Masters felt preordained. The amazement comes not from how well Woods played, but the way he could carry this burden of expectation from August through April knowing anything short of winning that tournament would be labeled as a failure, and still arrive in Augusta ready to do it.

Privately, Woods was nearly silent about what lay ahead. He normally loved talking to his team about the upcoming majors, his goals, what they needed to do, but this time he was mum on the matter whenever Williams or Harmon brought it up. Woods is one of the great compartmentalizers in sports, and nothing about that lead-up indicated he was playing for one of the greatest achievements possible. It was just another major he wanted to win.

So, as he prepared to begin his campaign for a fourth consecutive major, he walked from the putting green to the first tee wearing a black Nike hat, black pants, a black sweater vest, and a gray shirt underneath.

Harmon, the man who worked with him as a teenager, who taught him how to elevate his game, who rebuilt his entire swing at the peak and then found a new peak even higher, put his arm around Woods before he teed off.

"It's your time, pal," Harmon said. "Just go get it done."

"I got this, Butchie."

Chapter Eleven

———

THE FINAL HURDLE

Tiger Woods played different tournaments than his competitors. Not literally. But at every event that was not one of the big four, Woods worried about one thing: getting ready for the four majors. He tried to win of course. He practiced for each non-major and lived in and died with each shot. He's that competitive. But in terms of how he played the course, he played an entirely different tournament.

When he went to the Memorial in 2000, he noticed the rough was grown to four inches in certain places and the greens were mighty firm. It all looked to be set up how Pebble Beach would be. "So I practiced hitting that little 'chop' shot from the rough, letting the ball feed to the hole.

It not only came in handy for me in the Memorial, which I won, but it was a big part of my arsenal during the Open victory."

He'd study where all the majors were and learn how to win there. He'd adjust the flight of the ball, the shape of his shots. He accepted the risk of how this might hurt him on a given course between the majors, because everything was about maximizing his game for those four weeks a year.

"There were times in '99 when he was winning tournaments not with any of the shots that were required to win that tournament," Harmon said. "He was hitting shots that the four majors were going to require."

So, from the moment he won the PGA Championship in August 2000, and even more so since the start of the 2001 season, the only thing that mattered was preparing for Augusta. And Augusta was a course that required more specific types of shots than most. He made sure he could draw the ball at will, because holes 2, 5, 9, 10, 13, and 14 all suited right-to-left movement off the tee. Two of the best at Augusta were always Mickelson and Bubba Watson, two lefties skilled at hitting a lefty cut with that same movement. He increased his ball flight for certain shots, as the wind is less of a factor at Augusta than many other venues, and being able to aim for spots instead of using the ground. He practiced certain specific shots like the awkward pitch into the short No. 3 or the high-arcing shots over raised bunkers like on 7, 9, 18, and others. It is a mental man's course. At random points throughout the year, Williams would stop Woods on the range and demand a particular shot for a particular hole at Augusta and he'd have to hit in on command.

But there was one shot he practiced most.

Part of the famous Amen Corner trio of holes on the back nine, No. 13 is known as Azalea for the some 1,600 azaleas flanking the south side of the hole. It's a long but reachable dogleg par 5, but it's most famous for two things. The fairway runs with a severe right-to-left slope where the overwhelming majority of approaches must be hit with the ball well above your feet, and that slope is heavily guarded by Rae's Creek, which runs all along the left of the fairway before cutting in front of the green to defend that green from any attempt that's too short.

The safe play is normally to hit a drive well to the right toward the trees and pine straw. It leaves a much farther shot to the green, but the land is flatter, the angle in is better, and you remove the risk of any damage along the left.

Woods' No. 1 focus in those eight months was to master a sweeping draw off the tee that could carry through the air right along the dogleg and down the slope to leave himself a short iron in to reach the green in two. He practiced it constantly. Williams said he hit it more than any other shot. But the irony was Woods generally was a conservative player in majors. He didn't take risks just to take them, and he was a master at course strategy. He was just so good that some of his shots looked riskier than they were. So, for all the practice he did, he didn't use that draw the first three days of the 2021 Masters. It didn't feel right.

But Woods always loved the old Player quote "The more I practice, the luckier I get." Woods was prepared for all scenarios. Eventually, that shot would be called into play.

———

With the entire world expecting him to run away with another major victory, Woods pushed his opening tee shot way right into the trees. With the ball standing on the pine straw and wildlife all around him, he had to take his medicine. He grabbed a 2-iron and punched it through the trees, rolling it into the bunker in front of the green.

Bogey.

He shot an opening round 70 (2-under par) to leave himself five shots back of the lead in 15th place. By no means was it a poor round, but in five professional Masters appearances, he'd never shot lower than 70 in the first round.

"This is a major championship," he said. "There's four days. Everyone knows—it's awfully hard to go out there and shoot in the mid-60s every day in a major."

One man who did was Chris DiMarco, a late-blooming thirty-year-old journeyman making his Masters debut. Little did anyone know that over the next six years he'd be as intertwined with Woods on a Sunday as anyone, losing a sudden death playoff to Woods at the 2005 Masters before another runner up to Woods at the 2006 Open Championship. DiMarco opened Thursday with a 7-under 65 for the solo lead and said, "You're not going to have things go your way all the time, and I had everything go my way today. I just hope it stays like that."

The next day, as Woods slammed his putter and walked off the 9th green with a frustrating bogey, he passed an eighty-seven-year-old Sam Snead sitting next to the path in a red sweater and a straw hat. It was less than fifty years earlier when Ben Hogan was the only other man to win three consecutive professional majors in 1953 and he went for a fourth straight the next April, just like Woods. It was Snead who took him down in a playoff at that 1954 Masters to end the streak. It made it almost ominous as Woods passed him.

But Woods thrived that Friday. He birdied four of the first eight holes, including a beautiful second shot that rolled off the mounds to reach the par 5 eighth hole in two to set up birdie. He shot a 66, lifting himself from 15th to tied for 2nd, two shots back of DiMarco, who refused to go away.

"Woods, Duval, DiMarco. Do you belong in that group?" a reporter asked DiMarco.

"Well, I guess I do this week," DiMarco said. "Sure. I mean, why not? Before Woods and Duval were Woods and Duval they had to get there somehow, right? Maybe this is my week to get there."

The stage was set for a perfect weekend in Augusta. You had your Cinderella story in DiMarco. You had Woods going for the slam. Mickelson, still searching for his first major, was tied with Woods at 8-under. Duval was still going for his major title, too, and was three back at 7-under. Add in future and past major winners like Angel Cabrera, Lee Janzen, Mark Calcavecchia, and José María Olazábal. But it was all about Woods, and Mickelson couldn't be ignored.

"I don't think there has ever been a better opportunity for me to break through and win a major at this point," Mickelson said. "I'm playing well and I've learned to play smarter around this course. I think this weekend provides the best opportunity for me. I hope [Woods and I] have a chance to go head-to-head on Sunday."

And while golf history is littered with Woods' heroics, Saturday was about Woods hanging on while the field cratered around. He looked different from the previous three majors. While Pebble and St Andrews were blowouts and Valhalla looked like Woods having as much competitive fun as ever, Saturday in Augusta, Woods looked a different type of focused. Not robotic and machinelike as we're used to. It was a look of intensity, as if he felt the severity of the moment, felt the stars on his heels and knew he needed to lock in.

As he made the turn, he played simple par golf just 1-under par. Cabrera took control of the lead with an early run. Mickelson and DiMarco remained ahead of him, too. He'd won three major blowouts. He won another in a duel. But to win this, he'd have to rise through a star-studded back for the first time.

On 11, Woods hit a long, breaking putt curled into the hole as he lifted his entire putter up above his head. His face still didn't move, but his raised arm ignited the crowd around Amen Corner.

As he stood in the 14th fairway, he trailed Cabrera by two. Mickelson and DiMarco remained one ahead. He had to make a run. And seemingly at the same exact time across the Georgia pines, Cabrera hit his second shot on 15 into the water while Woods hit a perfect iron shot mere feet from the hole. Meanwhile, Mickelson put his approach on 14 short, rolling back down the hill. He could have saved par, but he got creative with a flop shot that once again fell slightly short and rolled the twenty-five feet back down the hill.

"I felt like the shot I played was not an unintelligent shot," he said. "It didn't come off that badly. It just was 30 feet and I three-putted."

In the span of minutes, Cabrera double bogeyed. Mickelson double bogeyed. And Woods birdied. It was practically a five-shot swing, Woods jumping into the lead while Cabrera and Mickelson fell behind. Woods then birdied 15 to get to 12-under for the day for the solo 54-hole lead, but Mickelson was able to birdie 17 and 18 to get within 1.

Mickelson got exactly what he wanted. He admitted all week he wanted to be in the final group with Tiger. He wanted his first major to come going head-to-head with the best.

Mickelson was the one who ended Woods' six-tournament win streak in 2000. He was the one who snagged the Tour Championship during Woods' greatest season. And now, he had a chance to rob him of a Grand Slam with a chance for his own personal breakthrough.

"I wanted to be playing with him," he said. A few minutes later, he added, "I desperately want this. I've been dreaming of this day."

Reporters kept pressing Woods to lean into the moment. No. 1 vs. No. 2 for the green jacket. Duval, Els, Calcavecchia, DiMarco, all on their tails, too. One more round for the Grand Slam, or whatever you wanted to call it. It was content gold. He wouldn't give in.

"Come on," the reporter playfully pleaded. "Give us something better than that. This is something a lot of us may never see again in our lifetime if you win again tomorrow. Has that entered into your mind?"

"I hope you live a little longer, then," Woods said to a room of laughter.

As the sun went down at Augusta National, the only people left to watch were Woods and Harmon, alone on the practice green. There were only eighteen holes left from eternity.

———

He had a bounce in his step that day, like there was nothing left to prove, like anything that would unfold that day was already determined, a practice-obsessed freak of nature believing anything decided that Sunday in Augusta was a result of the twenty-five years leading in. And for twenty-five years, Tiger Woods had been building to this moment.

He stayed steady as he opened with a bogey. He seemed fine as he parred four straight. He did not worry when the roars kept rising two groups ahead for Duval's four-straight birdies to take the lead. And then, the shots he'd been practicing for eight months came to him.

Like on 7, where he had to hit one of those high-arcing shots with no spin over the steep bunkers. He stuck it five feet past the hole where it stayed eight feet from the hole. He sunk his birdie putt and practically hopped to the hole as it went in, like a mini version of walk in on 16 at Valhalla.

Tiger joked once that he's been accused of hitting shots into trouble on purpose just to make a heroic recovery. They thought he just wanted the rush and the challenge.

"They were only partly right," he said. "I would never intentionally hit into trouble, but I must admit to seeing opportunity where others might not."

He said this while talking about the 8th hole, a par 5 where he left himself an awkward shot on a fairway downslope just off the other side of the green from the pin. Most normal people chip from there, accepting the risk of the lie and possibly butchering it. Not Woods. He hit an aggressive, powerful flop that landed right at the pin and rolled a few feet away. He made that birdie, too. He was tied with Duval with Mickelson one back.

He stayed calm again when his approach into 9 up the massive hill spun back off the front and down onto the slope. He played what he called a "little skippy spinner" to six feet from the pin to save par.

Woods and Duval remained tied, Mickelson two back, when they went to the 13th hole. It was time to finally hit the shot he'd been practicing.

Mickelson hit a perfect drive with his lefty cut to dead center of the fairway.

"Tiger decided that was the perfect time to play a little mind game with Phil," Williams said. Woods pulled out his 3-wood, not driver, and hit that sweeping hook he'd been waiting to use. For the previous two months, he spent a little extra time on each practice tee with that exact shot in his mind's eye. Woods says he doesn't consciously change his mechanics for certain swings. It's all by feel. So, his last thought before he took the club back was just "draw."

"The ball not only turned the corner," Woods recalled, "it didn't stop rolling until it came to rest in a perfect lie, 183 yards from the green."

It ended up some twenty yards past Mickelson's shot with a driver. Mickelson seemed dejected. Phil, always a gregarious character, asked Woods if he always hits it that long with his 3-wood. Woods, ready to dig a knife in, said, "No, further than that." They both birdied the hole, Mickelson remaining two back while Woods regained the solo lead.

He went to the 15th hole still in a three-way duel for the Masters. The crowd reached massive levels around him. But he was used to that. He was used to pandemonium. He was used to his peripheral vision being filled with thousands of people. But the skills going back to the Navy course with Earl or the psychological sessions with Jay Brunza taught him how to remove any and all distractions. They taught him focus. And as he prepared to hit that all-essential drive on 15—a par 5 with a green guarded by water where the location of your drive is so important—the crowd went quiet.

He began a full backswing and made his move down to hit the ball when amid the silence the sound of a clicking camera caught his attention. Who knows what was more impressive: The fact that he could hear the click while so focused on his drive with four holes to go in the Masters? The way his brain moved so quickly that while on the downswing he could process the sound of the click and still think to stop it at all? Or the fact that Woods had such physical ability he could stop his swing in a millisecond?

"I'm glad I did," he said, "or I might not have gotten that second green jacket."

Mickelson birdied 15 to get within one, while Woods made a rare mistake. He missed a makeable birdie that would have essentially sealed victory, considering Duval was in the process of bogeying 16 after missing the green.

Woods just stared at the ball. He didn't show anger, something he's not afraid to do. He didn't act exasperated. He just stared at it. Then, he slowly, deliberately picked it up and walked to 16. But still, he never picked his head up. It stayed down the entire walk, talking to himself. "Forget that hole. You have three holes to play. Let's go ahead and make one birdie coming in."

No. 16 is a short, beautiful par 3 with a large body of water in front and along the left of the green, but most of the strategy of the hole involves the large right-to-left slope on the right side of the green for the Sunday pin tucked in the back left above a bunker. Some of the most memorable shots in Masters history involve playing that slope to the hole, and Mickelson hit a 7-iron to the right of the green, planning to play that slope. Unfortunately, it stuck on the top of the slope and never moved down. Woods' shot had the same plan and landed *maybe* one foot left of Mickelson's, but that one foot was enough to roll down the hill for a far more manageable straight, uphill putt.

Mickelson had to line up his putt practically facing away from the hole, and it was too difficult. He left it ten feet from the hole, where he missed that par putt. Right then, Mickelson lost his chance at the Masters. Duval still trailed by one.

Playing 18 two groups ahead, Duval hit a beautiful uphill shot for a close birdie putt. Once again, Tiger heard the roar. Of course he did. In his mind, he thought he needed to birdie 17 to win this. But he left his approach too far right, rolling off the edge of the green. He nearly holed out his chip, but it just missed to ultimately par. He remained 15-under while Duval set up his birdie putt.

"There he is," Nantz said of Duval on the broadcast. "He's played his heart out today."

But Duval flew it past the hole. Behind his large, dark black shades, nobody could see what he was feeling or thinking. He went to tap in his par, again knowing he might have just lost his chance at the Masters. Woods just needed to par.

A bogey would send it to a playoff still, but "this was not a time to play defensively," Woods said. He made it this far. He won three majors. He won countless events. He wasn't going to just survive this. He was going to win it.

Woods bombed a driver, committing to "ripping the ball almost as hard as I could." He held his finish far longer than normal. Some might have wondered if he was savoring the moment, but no. He was locked on his ball, concerned he faded it too much around the corner of the dogleg right. There are trees along the right, and Woods sincerely didn't know where it landed. He even grimaced as he began his walk.

He walked down the large hill and back up the up-slope still unsure. He got closer and saw a ball sitting in the right-side rough and his heart sank. Fortunately, it was Mickelson's. He kept on walking, and there he found his Nike ball sitting pretty in the fairway seventy-eight yards from the hole. That moment might have been the first time it occurred to Woods he was about to win. He and Williams gave each other a slightly delayed low-five.

"Man, was I relieved—and excited."

He put his approach right into the center of the green. It was over. He walked up the hill to a standing ovation and took off his hat to display his sweaty buzzed hair. For the first time, he looked tired.

But instead of two-putting for par and a Masters victory, Woods went ahead and made the birdie putt, launching his fist into the air.

Four majors were played between June 2000 and April 2001. Tiger Woods had won them all.

———

Chapter Twelve

CALL IT WHAT
YOU WANT

His entire life had been about the next shot. The next hole. The next round. The next year. It had been twenty-five years of building what Tiger Woods would become, and suddenly the fully realized version Tiger Woods was here. It was no longer about his potential. It was no longer about his future. The little boy who worked with his dad in the garage stood on the green at Augusta National reaching the pinnacle of the sport that may never be matched.

Woods walked to the side of the 18th green to allow

Mickelson to finish out his round, took his hat off, and scanned the scenery atop the hill. Then his eyes closed and he turned and put his face into his chest. Almost like he was mad at himself, because he unraveled. He covered his face with his black Nike hat to hide his feelings from the world.

When he won the US Open, he smiled. When he won the Open Championship, he let out a somber "wow." When he won the PGA, he gave a face of exhausted relief. But he never celebrated for long. He was back on the range the next day. Earl and Tiger's motto was "We came, we won, we got the fuck out of town." But at least for the time being, there was nothing left to chase.

It finally hit him.

"I just started thinking, you know, I don't have any more shots to play," Woods said. "I'm done."

"It was just a weird feeling, because, you know, when you are focused so hard on each and every shot, you kind of forget everything else. When I didn't have any more shots to play, that's when I started to realize what I had done."

Woods embraced Williams and walked through the crowd to find both his parents waiting, smiling and celebrating with each other. They had been separated for years, but they cried and Earl made a fittingly crude yet sentimental joke about the creation of Tiger Woods. "I guess that was one lucky night, huh?" Woods wrapped his arms around Earl, and then he made his way to Kultida. His smile never seemed larger.

What was once a myth in the golf game had actually happened. No matter the semantics of which title you decide to call it, Woods won four majors in a row. Here was a young man who before he played a single major set his sights on breaking Nicklaus' record of eighteen. Who won the Masters by a record margin at twenty. Who reached the career Grand Slam sooner than anyone in history. Who played the greatest individual major performance ever at the US Open. Who set the lowest scoring major ever at the Open Championship. Who won one of the greatest duels of all time in the PGA. And then, he really did it. He became the first golfer to ever hold all four professional majors at the same time. Nicklaus and Palmer never won more than two in a year. The people he measured himself against had never done what he just did.

And it was only boosted by the different ways he did it. Many majors come and go and are part of the history books but not quite *remembered*. None of these four will be. And each one displayed another element of what made

Woods one of the most special athletes in recent memory. At one of the toughest tests in all of golf at Pebble Beach, he annihilated the field with steady discipline. At St Andrews, he didn't find a single one of the iconic bunkers while playing all-around perfect golf. So, when some wondered if he could only win blowouts, he won in an old-fashioned duel down to the finish. And at Augusta, he showed he could hang in the middle of a crowded, star-studded leaderboard and break through. What was left to test?

He admitted that when he won in 1997, he was young. He was naive. The importance of what he accomplished slightly went over his head.

"This year, I understand. I've been around the block. I've witnessed a lot of things since that year. You know, I have better appreciation for winning a major championship, and to win it—to win four of them in succession, it's just—it's hard to believe, really, because there's so many things that go into winning a major championship."

Duval and Mickelson finally showed up to take Woods down to the wire. They did their part. And Duval's 14-under would have won fifty-nine of the previous sixty-five Masters. Mickelson's performance would have won plenty, as well. Els finished second place to Woods more than anyone.

Yet whenever it seemed like he was mortal—when he spent two years changing his swing, when he went winless for eight tournaments—we learned it was because he was doing something to widen the gap even more. *Sports Illustrated*'s Rick Reilly put it best: "They have no chance. They'll never have a chance. What's worse is they now realize that every time they think Woods is slipping, it's only because he's up nights building something even better in the garage."

The father who'd privately been out of the picture for months could finally enjoy his moment in the public eye. He later said: "Words cannot describe the pleasure and pride I felt when he came into my arms as he walked off the 18th green that Sunday afternoon, the sun sinking behind those huge pine trees. Four years earlier it was a similar scene after Tiger won his initial Masters during his first full year on tour. This time was different. This time I embraced a grown-up who had tried on the title of best in the world and found it a perfect fit. I said to him, 'You pulled it off. Now you really are in the history books. I love you.'"

Soon the pontificators questioned if this really qualified as a Grand Slam. The rational ones rolled their eyes and said who cared. It was a made-up designation created to quantify something special that happened seventy years before. And that something special was being the champion of all four majors at once.

Yes, Vijay Singh won the 2000 Masters. But in that moment, Vijay Singh was not the champion of the Masters. As Singh ceremonially placed the jacket on Woods, and then as he kept doing it over and over again because the photographers wanted more shots of it, it cemented that there was not a single other men's major champion in all of golf.

Harmon got into an argument about it with a reporter he'd rather not name. "Let me put it in a perspective you can understand," Harmon told him. "There's never been a human being walking on the planet Earth that's just done what this guy has just done. So why don't you just fucking call it what you like?"

Many took Hootie Johnson's approach, focusing on what was accomplished and not what wasn't.

"To me," Earl said that day, "it's like when a scientist discovers a star. He discovers it, he gets his name on it. Nobody's ever done this before, so Tiger should get his name on it."

To this day, it is remembered as the Tiger Slam.

———

As people look back on Tiger Woods' career, they have an ability to break it into eras. Some break it into swings. Some break it into coaches. But Woods always had the ability to redefine himself and rise again, such a large part of why he's one of the icons most ingrained into American sports history.

There was the skinny kid launching golf balls with raw, unharnessed power. The one who won every U.S. Amateur and ran away with the 1997 Masters. He had no fear, yet he wasn't always able to control himself. His rounds were more erratic. As were his tournaments. As was his life. He put himself on too many advertisements. He spread himself too thin. He said things in magazine interviews that damaged his reputation. But god, was he fun?

There was Tiger 2.0. He was the perfectly oiled machine. He fixed his swing with Harmon to create something that most professionals to this day call the greatest swing of all time. He was a little bulkier and stronger but not too much. He didn't hit it quite as far, but he had more control. His play showed up practically every single week, to the point he could win six tournaments in a row. He could win ten tournaments in a year. He could win four consecutive majors and change golf forever. And this version of Woods was more controlled all around. He was not yet living a lifestyle that put him in the tabloids. He cut out most of the attention seekers in his inner circle. He kept his interviews dry and never revealed too much. He was unreachable, but that combined with the constant allure of his abilities made us reach out for him so much more. It was his least troubled time, but also the formation of his compartmentalized, private mega stardom that led to his downfall.

But, as you all know, this was not the end of Woods. Far from it. The things that propelled Woods to such great heights were the things that slowly, and then all so quickly, led to his downfall. And they were also the things that could bring him back to the top once more late in his career.

Of the many things that connect Woods and Michael Jordan, one of them is the compulsion for more. And Woods had a hard time accepting complacency.

He was exhausted after the 2001 Masters and the Tiger Slam, and he won just two more tournaments that year. His best major finish was T12. In 2002, he won the Masters and the US Open to increase that major tally to eight by age twenty-six. But so much of his circle was changing. He and Jagoda, a calming presence through 2000, split at some point after Valhalla, notably during that infamous eight weeks without a win. He met Elin Nordegren, a Swedish au pair for golfer Jesper Parnevik, in late 2001. By 2004, they were married.

He also split with maybe the steadiest presence through his rise, aside from Kultida. Even Earl Woods had been pushed out of the picture by 2000, but Butch Harmon remained. But by 2001, a tension developed between him and Woods. Some books and reports place that tension from Harmon focusing on "maintenance" as Woods was the best player in the world without a peer for at least three years. But, like Jordan, Woods needed something to chase. Maintenance wouldn't work for him. Steve Williams wrote in his autobiography that it had more to do with Harmon taking attention, a common thread in Woods' breakups, from Fluff Cowan to Hughes Norton to his old lawyer John Merchant and potentially to even Earl.

"Tiger would hear him on TV saying, 'When I was with Tiger . . . When I did this with Tiger . . . I was practicing with Tiger the other day . . .' Tiger felt like Butch was trading on his name, taking advantage of their association," Williams said. But Williams said Woods never spoke to Harmon about any of this. He simply froze him out for a year.

"Tiger is not a normal person when it comes to relationships," Williams continued. "His default mode is to cut all communication and avoid any conflict when he gets annoyed with someone. If he thought you'd said something or done something, his reaction was to put the mute on."

By the 2002 PGA Championship, their relationship was over. Woods ignored Harmon when he went to speak to him a few days later.

It's difficult and unfair to assign meaning to each moment in a complicated life, but his breakup with Harmon coincided with a tough stretch in Woods' career. He didn't win any majors in 2003 or 2004, going ten majors without a win for the first time since 1997 to 1999.

This next era is what some label as the Haney era. Or Tiger 3.0. He was a little bigger and bulkier than before. The injuries began to pile up. He started working with famous swing coach Hank Haney, leading to another entirely new swing. He got married. His habits with women outside of marriage picked up steam, as well. He launched an obsession with the military and told Williams he wanted to quit golf to become a Navy SEAL. He was at his most volatile but also at his most fascinating.

Woods returned to form, winning the Masters and Open Championship in 2005, a dominant season that DataGolf considers the third best statistical season of all time. That included a chip in at the Masters on 16 that may go down as Woods' most famous shot.

In May 2006, Earl died of kidney failure. That only fueled Woods' emotional attachment to his Navy SEAL dream as he spent time training with the SEALs instead of focusing on golf. But two months later, Woods went to Royal Liverpool to win the Open Championship at 18-under in one of his greatest career performances. Right as he won, he melted into Williams' arms, burying his head into Williams' armpit as he cried like a baby.

"I just wish he could have seen it one more time," Woods said.

While Woods' private life seemed to be at its most chaotic—cheating on Elin with other women, losing his father, and attempting to leave it all for the military—Woods' career reached its second peak. Under Haney's instruction, he won his twelfth major at the PGA Championship that fall and won eight of the fifteen tournaments he entered. There's an argument his 2006 season was even better than 2000. He added another at the 2007 PGA and in 2008 won his fourteenth major in arguably his most memorable major of all. With a broken leg, Woods willed himself to a playoff with Rocco Mediate at the 2008 US Open at Torrey Pines. It still wasn't decided by an 18-hole playoff, and Woods won in sudden death. He and Nordegren had two kids, Sam and Charlie.

From a public perspective, 2008 was the absolute height of Woods' success and popularity. He was on pace to shatter Nicklaus' records. He had a seemingly perfect life.

But that essentially marked the end of the third Woods era. The leg injury ended his 2008 season. When he returned, he still thrived, winning seven tournaments in 2009 and finishing top 10 at three of four majors. He just didn't win any, including the 2009 PGA Championship against Y. E. Yang, which symbolized the first time Woods ever lost a major with a 54-hole lead.

That Thanksgiving, police were called when Woods attempted to flee his home and crashed his car as Nordegren confronted him about his numerous affairs. Thus launched one of the larger tabloid scandals in recent memory, with Woods' extracurricular activities becoming a top story for the better part of a year. He and Nordegren divorced. Many of his sponsors dropped him. Woods didn't win an event in 2010, and for the first time in five years he lost the world No. 1 crown.

Tiger 4.0 was a stranger period. He and Haney split. A year later, he split with Williams, too. The core pieces of his original rise were all gone, and he began working with coach Sean Foley. He even regained his form. After three years without it, he took back the world No. 1 spot for sixty weeks straight. He won three times in 2012 and five times in 2013. But still no majors. He was stuck at fourteen.

Then, his body gave out. Back surgeries. Wrist injuries. His hip. He played very little golf from 2014 to 2017, only returning to a normal season in 2018. But also in May 2017, Woods was arrested in Florida for a DUI. He was asleep in his stationary car left in a bike lane. He said he was on prescription drugs, and it felt like Woods' entire life was falling apart.

He got help and found a new circle of friends for support. His golf game found another wind and he won the Tour Championship in 2018.

But it was in April 2019 that the comeback of Tiger Woods seemed to come full circle. Twenty-two years after his first Masters win, this time with a hobbled body after countless surgeries, Woods returned to Augusta and shocked the world to win the Masters. He played steady, intelligent golf while the field made mistakes around him. When he won, he launched both arms up into the air and screamed with both eyes shut tight. It marked the final reminder that Woods is not like normal people. He can push his body to do things most cannot. He can train his brain to compartmentalize, focus, and withstand pain at unheard-of levels. And he could still play golf.

When he won that Masters in 1997, the famous photo cemented in history was of Tiger and Earl hugging to validate twenty years of work together. This time, Tiger was a forty-three-year-old father of two running into the arms of his children, Charlie and Sam, and, of course, Kultida.

But the story of Tiger Woods is never settled. In February 2021, during his signature Genesis Invitational that he hosts but wasn't playing in, Woods survived a terrifying single-car rollover crash in California that knocked him unconscious. His leg was broken in multiple places, and officials said he was lucky to be alive. It was widely assumed in that moment that he'd never walk again.

Still, he did not fade away. Soon videos surfaced of Woods hitting the ball at his home. Soon he was walking rounds with Charlie, an aspiring golfer himself. He returned to play the 2022 Masters, and inexplicably he made the cut while hobbling around the course. His walking looked labored. Each step was followed by a slight grimace. But he knew how to play Augusta. He knew how to golf. He went on to make the cut at the PGA Championship the next month, only to withdraw due to his body being unable to hold up at Southern Hills. He missed the cut at the Open.

But what may, in its own strange way, be the most impressive accomplishment on a golf course for Tiger Woods is that he returned the next year to make the Masters cut again. Again, he returned in 2024, and this time he made the cut by five shots. Despite Woods' body taking more damage than possibly any golfer in history, he made the cut at twenty-four consecutive Masters. It was a new record.

Nowadays, Woods is primarily an executive. He's a billionaire businessman, but in the midst of the PGA Tour's ongoing war with LIV Golf, a rival league funded by the Public Investment Fund of Saudi Arabia, Woods was given a permanent, non-elected seat on the PGA Tour Policy Board. He has become the leading voice of players as golf changes its structure, and in many ways he is one of the most powerful figures in all of golf.

Yet no matter how much Woods changes, no matter how much his body gets fused or filled with metal, there is a constant in his life. He still finds the most comfort and solace on a golf course. He still finds happiness in the solitude of practice.

"But the joy is different now," he said, Woods finding himself reminiscent in a way he never would have been twenty years before. "I've been able to spend more time with my son, and we've been able to create our own memories out there. And to share some of the things that my dad, what I experienced with my dad, the late-night putting or practice sessions that we did at the Navy Golf Course, I'm doing with my son. It's incredible."

He spent thirty minutes talking at the Masters press conference, telling old stories about learning the course from Fred Couples and Raymond Floyd, how he hit that chip in 2005 or how he was starting to share his knowledge with younger players like Tom Kim or Scottie Scheffler.

He could tell these stories, because he finally reached the point in life where it wasn't about what came next. It was OK to look back.

So, we look back to that golfer, invincible and fearless, alone on a driving range searching for perfection. He was the best player in the world, but he wanted more. And then he found it.

"Butchie, I got it," he said.

And then, we saw greatness.

ACKNOWLEDGMENTS

This book began with an idea and a leap of faith. The great editor Sean Desmond took a chance on a then-twenty-nine-year-old reporter who'd never written a book, much less planned to write one. And he gave that reporter the runway to take a chance but also laid out that runway carefully with comfort, advice, and the tools to actually write this thing. Sean and the greater team involved didn't just treat this book like a one-off project. They encouraged me to begin a new chapter, and for that I am grateful.

The other person who made this book happen with Sean was Mark Tavani. Calling Mark an agent feels disingenuous. Mark is an incredible editor and creative mind who was the man editing all proposals and talking through narrative and structure the entire process. This book does not happen without Mark, both because he was the first person to reach out, take a chance, and see if I was interested in writing a book, and because his counsel helped put this whole thing together.

A large thank-you to the greater HarperCollins team. Not just Sean, but to Jackie Quaranto, who did so much of the work and dealt with my scattered brain to actually take the book from submitted words to a fully realized product. Jackie is the real MVP. And a large thank-you to the behind-the-scenes stars like Becca Putnam in marketing the book, Kate D'Esmond for her work in publicity, the awesome production team of Frieda Duggan and Michael Siebert, and of course interior designer Kyle O'Brien.

I'd be remiss if I didn't acknowledge my editor at *The Athletic*, Hugh Kellenberger, who took my first call asking what he thought of me writing a book on the side and answered with excitement, not concern. He was patient when I needed to take time away to write, and he was a sounding board as I attempted to figure this project out. Hugh gave me my first job out of college as a general assignment writer at the *Clarion-Ledger* in Jackson, Mississippi, and here we are eight years later living the dream. Hugh, thank you for everything.

But most importantly, this book was written the same year my wife and I spontaneously decided to elope in the Scottish Isles and finally get married. I don't know if I'd ever advise anybody to write a book the same year they're planning an international wedding and starting a new role at work, but Clare was the glue that got me through it. She was kind, supportive, and patient on the longest days and nights. She was firm when I needed a kick to keep going. And she was so insightful when I needed the thoughts of somebody I trust. I love you, Clare, and what a year we'll remember forever.

Oh, and to our English bulldogs Lilly and Delilah. We lost Delilah right as this book was beginning, and Lilly, a sixty-pound block of mass that believes she's a lap dog, insisted on sitting on our laps and serving as a quasi-table as Clare and I tried to work. Bulldogs make life better.

INDEX

INDEX

INDEX

Player, Gary, 67–68, 119, 174
Players Championship, 171–172
Price, Nick, 96–97
Public Investment Fund, 206
Pumpkin Ridge, 142–144
putting average, 116–117

race/racism
    on golf courses, 81–82
    "Hello World" ad and, 81–82
    Tiger's hope to transcend, 89–90
    Tiger's views on, 83–86
    Zoeller incident, 84–85
Rahm, Jon, 52, 125
Ray, Justin, 58–59
red polo, as Tiger's signature shirt, 54, 111, 136
Reilly, Rick, 160, 196
repetitive stimuli, 19–20
Roberts, Clifford, 118
Roberts, Jimmy, 52–53, 57–58, 170–172
Robinson, Jackie, 21
role model expectations, 87–89
Rushin, Steve, 96

Salzman, Leon, 26
Sarazen, Gene, 67

Sargent, Gordon, 125
Schauffele, Xander, 108, 133
Scheffler, Scottie, 23, 52, 115, 168
Scott, Adam, 40–41, 112–113
Scott, Steve, 143–144
Scotty Cameron Newport 2 GSS putter, 8
Singh, Vijay, 115–116, 197
Smith, Gary, 82
Smith, LaBradford, 55
Snead, Sam, 68, 180–181
Spieth, Jordan, 17, 68, 116, 125
St Andrews. *See also* Open Championship
    beauty of, 98
    bunkers, 91–94, 195
    caddying, 94–95
    Duval and, 98–100
    final round, 99–102
    Hell Bunker, 92–93, 97–98
    sandy depressions, 91
    Swilken Bridge, 101
    Tiger receiving the Claret Jug, 102
    Tiger's best shot of his career at, 97–99
    Tiger's win at, 100–101

ABOUT THE AUTHOR

Brody Miller is a reporter at *The Athletic,* where he covers golf and college football. He lives in New Orleans with his wife, Clare, and his bulldog Lilly.